NEW YORK

MYTHS & LEGENDS

NEW YORK

MYTHS & LEGENDS

THE TRUE STORIES BEHIND HISTORY'S MYSTERIES

SECOND EDITION

FRAN CAPO

Globe
Pequot

Guilford, Connecticut

Globe
Pequot

An imprint of The Rowman & Littlefield Publishing Group, Inc.
4501 Forbes Blvd., Ste. 200
Lanham, MD 20706
www.rowman.com

Distributed by NATIONAL BOOK NETWORK

British Library Cataloguing-in-Publication Information available

Library of Congress Cataloging-in-Publication Data available

ISBN 978-1-4930-3984-5 (paperback)
ISBN 978-1-4930-3985-2 (e-book)

♾™ The paper used in this publication meets the minimum requirements of American National Standard for Information Sciences—Permanence of Paper for Printed Library Materials, ANSI/NISO Z39.48-1992.

CONTENTS

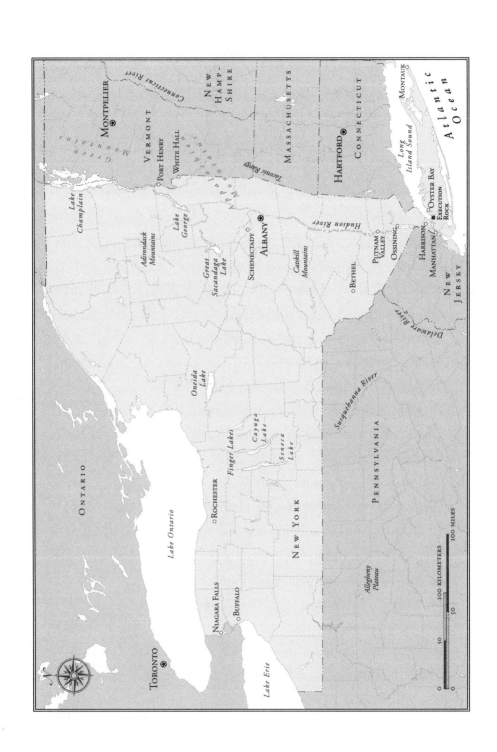

Acknowledgments

New York Myths and Legends is the second edition of my original book, Myths and Mysteries of New York, making this my twentieth book! Yes, I've been quite a busy writer and loving it. The first edition of Myths and Mysteries of New York was my fifteenth book, and it never ceases to amaze me how many people help along the way. In this second edition I'd like to thank R. Marchan from the Lower Hudson Valley Paper for giving me a heads up that the Leatherman's gravesite had been moved. I'd also like to Craig Morrison of Historical Significant Structures, Inc., a non-profit 501(c)(3) organization that now is in charge of Execution Rock Island. Craig gave me the photo for the chapter, and since it was past the overnight season to stay there, he got me in touch with Linda Dianto, director of the National Lighthouse Museum on Staten Island. They had one more "haunted boat tour" going out this season past Execution Rock, but unfortunately I got a stand up gig that night so I was unable to go, but for those who ever are interested you can get some really cool facts from them. (By the way, both places could use donations, so if you like visiting places like these please consider going on tours with them or donating to their cause!) I also like to thank Tom Renner, who arranged for a sailboat for me to go out to Execution Island, in case I wasn't able to get a photo another way!

As for the Stone Chambers chapter (14), I'd like to thank my two neighbors Ellen and Artie (who I call Barry) Gershman for introducing me to Polly Midgley, coordinator of NEARA.org (the New England Antiquities Research Association) that finances several scientific studies on the chambers and gave me an great interview and other names of people to contact to verify information.

Thanks also to my wonderful friend and housekeeper, Justina Cuomo, who without her my house would not have been kept clean while I spent endless hours working on this book.

Thanks to Courtney Oppel, my wonderful editor, for reaching out to me and asking if I'd be interested in doing a second edition, to which I responded, "YES!!!"—but I need more money! LOL. (Obviously we worked out a deal or you wouldn't be holding this book in your hands!)

As for my first edition published back in 2011, those acknowledgments still stand and they were:

First to Meredith Rufino of Globe Pequot—thank you for asking me to work on this fascinating series, for giving your great input, and for editing skills that made me look good once again. Thanks also to my first edition project editor, Meredith Dias, for working on the final manuscript.

Next up, my darling son, Spencer (yes, I said darling), who still lets me read each chapter to him as I finish it, then promptly calls his friends (and now also his fiancée, Heather) and says, "Hey, we gotta check out this place that my mom just wrote about!" Now that is loyalty! Also thanks to him for taking pictures of the alligators, the Dakota, and for exploring the Leather Man's cave with me.

Then there is Steve, who was my boyfriend of eleven years when I wrote the first edition and now is my husband, (We finally figured after sixteen years we knew each other well enough to tie the knot.) Although he still complains that my writing takes me away from our together time, he is always the first to buy my books and give them as gifts to his clients—and he not only gave me the idea to do the chapters on Hell Gate and Typhoid Mary but also took me on his boat to photograph the places. We went through treacherous waters, circled islands, and almost had the Coast Guard chase us away, but all in the name of research! This time around with my second edition, he came with me to photograph the Leatherman's new gravesite, despite a torrential downpour in the cemetery. (I think it was the Leatherman saying, "Will people ever leave me alone!")

A very special thanks to my dear friend and then-assistant, Dale Kilian, who was my right-hand man on the field runs, taking photos and flips, setting up interviews with the experts, protecting me from ghosts, and doing the maps. I also appreciate that he always cheered me on as I approached a deadline. You're one of a kind! (And still a cheerleader in my life!)

Thanks to all the librarians, historical societies, and docents who helped, especially docent Joanne Kessler from Skene Manor, who let me use my flip camera (those were big back then) to record the entire story of the ghost hostess. Thanks also to Donald Fiorino, Dottie Hart, and Kay Styles. Special thanks to Travis Greenlee, Ellen Easton, Richie Magic (RIP) Gemini, George Bettinger (RIP) Al Cole, Art Noble, Donna Drake from Live it

Up! TV, Kim Orlando, and Nancy Lombardo for enthusiastically promoting my work.

Thanks to comic Max Dolcelli for telling me about McGurk's Suicide Hall.

And to my now step-daughter, Jamie Davis, who at midnight in a kitchen said, "You have to include a chapter about Buckout Road!"

Finally, thanks to you, the readers. It's your enthusiasm and quest for information that keeps me writing and employed, not to mention buying my books that caused it to go into a second edition!) As always, if you like the book, please buy more, spread the word on ALL forms of social media, create a viral meme, hold a banner, give them as gifts, tell your friends, your family, your Facebook buddies, the FedEx man—just let them know it's out there, or send them to my website, www.francapo.com. I'd truly appreciate it and so would my publisher.

INTRODUCTION

Being a six-time world record holder, best known as the *Guinness Book of Records'* fastest talking woman (not to mention other crazy records, like book signings atop Kilimanjaro and at the wreck site of the *Titanic*), I have some wild world record–holding friends. Friends like Throwdini, the world's fastest knife thrower (who was also the minister at our wedding and threw knives at us during the ceremony— yes, it was planned and that's a whole other story), and Ashrita Furman, who holds over one hundred simultaneous world records in all kinds of things from pogo-sticking up Mount Fuji, to skipping with a tiger, to making the world's biggest seesaw. The point is that we are all living proof of something my mom taught me—nothing is impossible—and what my dad taught me—that you always have to have the ability to laugh at yourself and the world.

So I approached this book with an open mind and sense of humor. In researching the myths and mysteries of New York, I could not always rely just on books. I often had to go into the trenches and talk to the neighborhood people to ask what they had seen, heard, and witnessed, and then I had to figure out which people I could believe, which people were nuts, and who was just looking for a fleeting moment of fame.

I also had to figure out what part of a story was legend, what was fact, and why the story still exists today. I had to remember what had and had not been discovered during the period I was investigating. For example, some crimes of the past remain unsolved because tools we take for granted today, like a police force or DNA testing, were unavailable at the time. Researching the unknown past, I found, is like investigative reporting. But I had to go one step further as I asked myself if I could stretch my mind and believe the unbelievable.

A place that is known for ghosts, murder, or the bizarre is not always a place you want to go to alone. So I often brought a trusted family member or friend to experience it with me. (Makes for a good photo album!) All the stories in this book fascinate me, but there are five behind-the-scenes experiences from my research adventures I'd like to tell you about.

CHAPTER 3: THE MONTAUK PROJECT

After all my research was done on this chapter, I went back to take a photo. With me was Dale Kilian and my good friend, journalist, and attorney Alan Chan. Alan was doing an article on me and wanted to shadow some of my activities. The night before, my then boyfriend Steve, Dale, and I looked at satellite photos to see what road would get us the closest to the SAGE radar. I also wanted to find an entranceway into the underground lab where the project took place.

We arrived at Camp Hero State Park at 10 a.m. and went to a private area on a dirt road. Dale and I weren't even out of the car for a minute when a security cop came along and said to us, "You know this is private property?" What do I say? "Hey, do you know anything about the time travel chair?" He would have locked me up immediately. So I said I was a history buff and wanted to get a picture of the SAGE radar. Then I asked if he knew anything about the Montauk Project. He immediately stiffened up. "Nope, no clue." I kept pushing and finally he said, "Go into town, there's a guy who works at a golf shop named Tom Dess. You might want to talk to him." I asked the officer's name, but he refused to give it.

We then went over to the public area of the park and scouted around. We saw a vandalized, fenced-off section. I wanted to go underneath and take a photo, but Alan advised me not to. We wound up wandering through the silent woods and found some out-of-place, massive rock pilings. We believed it was to cover up something underneath. Most other areas of the base were cemented shut with big warning signs. We also noticed that the security guards were following us. We picked up a pamphlet and found out that visitors needed to be careful of UXO— Unexploded Ordinances—in other words, land mines that may not have gone off. The pamphlet warned, "Do not move closer. Never transmit radio frequencies near UXO." And finally, "Don't worry: The public is not in danger."

Later that day we went to the Montauk Library. A very sweet librarian who did not want her name associated with the Montauk chapter helped us tremendously in finding articles in the library's files about government cover-ups and the like. We also searched for Tom Dess, but never found him.

A month later, Dale and I drove up to Cairo, New York, to interview Preston Nichols, engineer, author, lecturer, and foremost authority on the Montauk Project. I told Steve if I wasn't back by nightfall to assume I had time-traveled some place and to come find me.

Upon arrival we went into Nichols' home office, which had a vibrating musical bed with flashing fluorescent lights overhead in the middle of it. The bed was supposed to alter DNA, which is a whole other story (but, ironically, now I have a holistic healer, Ken Kobayashi, who uses a Quantum bed that is said to do the same thing, so maybe Nichols was onto something back then and ahead of his time!). Anyway, Nichols openly talked about his time travel experiences, his memory of his parallel lives, and the psychic and mind-altering experiments that were part of the Montauk Project. As an engineer Nichols had been involved in many other government projects in the past. He did not reveal names, but talked about quantum physics, radio waves, and a lot of heady technical stuff. I asked him outright if people thought he was a genius or a nut. He laughed and said, "Both." Then he added, "You have to understand those kind of theories to find these things plausible." The funny thing is I grew up with my mom teaching me about Wicca, the third eye, metaphysics, Egyptian flame rituals, Edgar Cayce, and the power of the mind; my classmates thought I was nuts. Clips of our interview are available on my YouTube channel, Fran Capo. I thanked Nichols for his time—in this dimension. I asked him to bring me back a lottery ticket next time he time-traveled. He looked at me as if I was nuts!

CHAPTER 6: THE MYSTERIOUS LEATHER MAN

The next behind-the-scenes story involves me trying to test my endurance. The Leather Man was a homeless man who walked a 365-mile route every thirty-four days dressed in heavy leather. I took my son, Spencer, on this sojourn. On my birthday I wanted to find one of the many caves the Leather Man stayed in on his trek. To do this we journeyed to Ward Pound Ridge Reservation. The man at the information counter gave us a map and explained in detail how to locate the cave. (Thank you!) It was a long trek, and the cave was not easy to find. Finally, we found it way on top of a huge hill. We hung out inside, looked around for the buried treasure, waited to see if his ghost would shoo us away, and then trekked back. I was tired from traveling to that one cave. How he did all of them in thirty-four days is amazing, and then repeated it over and over again! At some point I'm going to try his entire loop just to see how long it will take me to do it in shorts and a T-shirt. Then people can yell, "The fast talker is coming, the fast talker is coming!" Okay, maybe not.

I did have to update this story because almost a decade after he died they couldn't leave the poor guy alone. They dug up his grave and then moved it, all to examine his corpse and test his DNA to try to learn more about him. But a mystery occurred, which I won't tell you—you'll have to read the chapter. But I will say on the day I went to investigate this—this time with my husband, Steve—the moment we drove into the cemetery it started to pour. Coincidence? Who knows? That video is on Facebook if you would like to see it though, just in case you need to verify.

This story of the Leatherman so inspired me, that I penned a poem about him that I have added to the chapter and can also be read on my website, www.francapo.com.

CHAPTER 7: THE LAKE CHAMPLAIN MONSTER

My work on "Champ," the monster of Lake Champlain, was perfectly timed. While doing research for this chapter, I happened upon a press release that said the town of Port Henry holds a Champ Day celebration the first Saturday of every August, which was two days away. I called my friend, Lisa Wernick, and asked if she wanted to try to get photos of a sea monster. She was game.

We arrived in Port Henry around noon. There at the edge of this small, quaint town was a large sign with the names of dozens of upright citizens who had spotted Champ. After a few pictures we headed into town. The parade was already over and there were only about seven tents. We went into the library and met Mary Consadine, a spry, eighty-eight-year-old woman of many professions, including former trustee of Sherman Free Library for forty-eight years; third grade teacher; docent at the local iron ore museum; part owner of the church in town; and the list goes on. She invited us into her home and for several hours gave us the dirt on Champ, complete with newspaper clippings that were essential to my research. She believes there is something huge in that water and would like to know what it is before she leaves this planet.

Then we headed over to The Inn on the Library Lawn in Westport, a combination bookstore and B&B. The owners, Alexandria and Anthony Wheeler, have a hidden picture of Champ that his father-in-law, Gary Gorman, created. After a few calls, we got in touch with Gary's wife, Carol, who gave us permission to use this hysterical photo.

Determined to get photos of our own, Lisa and I headed to Lake Champlain at night, figuring that's when Champ might make an appearance. We threw some raisins in the water to bait him. (Hey, I never said I was an expert on what sea monsters eat; as long as it wasn't us I was happy.) Anyway, we didn't spot Champ but we did go country dancing that night. The next morning we got up at dawn to try again. We found out that the spot where we had stood the night before was only two feet deep. Unless Champ was a midget, chances are we weren't seeing him on this trip. But apparently since I wrote the first edition, many other people have seen him and even managed to capture him on film. I'll have to find out what bait they used.

CHAPTER 8: BIZARRE TALES OF BUCKOUT ROAD

This behind-the-scenes story takes us to Buckout Road in Westchester. My research led me to professional wrestler and Buckout expert Eric Pleska, aka Eric Tapout. After a one-hour late night phone chat on the multiple hauntings of Buckout Road, we decided to meet up one day at a Dunkin' Donuts in the area and he would give me a guided tour of Buckout. Unfortunately on that morning, construction made me detour, and I couldn't find where we were supposed to meet. Dale, my copilot, was with me, and my buddy Carson Tang was on the phone looking up all the Dunkin' Donuts in the area, trying to locate which one Eric was waiting at, but to no avail. Finally, we decided to just head over to the road and take some pictures.

When Dale and I got to the road, I saw a chained area that I remembered seeing on a YouTube video. On the other side of this chain was supposed to be the flesh-eating albino's house. I wanted to grab a picture. I parked my car and all of a sudden this man pulls up and says, "Can I help you?" He was saying that, but his body language said, "What the hell are you up to?" I told him I was looking for a Dunkin' Donuts. Then I finally blurted out, "I'm a writer, and I need to know the truth about Buckout Road." He rolled his eyes and said, "Follow me."

He drove into this narrow gravel road. I looked at Dale. "Okay, are we nuts following a guy we don't know into a back road off of the most haunted road in New York?" Dale shrugged and said, "Go with the adventure." Joe (who doesn't want his last name known) then brought us to his home. He took out a two-hundred-year-old map and some pictures. "The house I'm in used to be one of the three albino houses. Kids come here all the time looking to be spooked. I can tell you tons of stories of murders, suicides, and ghosts and I can give you names." And he did. Then he offered to take us in the backwoods to the haunted "Negro cemetery" as marked on the map. He said, "You know my wife would kill me if she knew I was doing this." I said, "Yeah, so would my boyfriend; he'd think I was nuts for going with a strange man into a desolate cemetery. How do I know you don't have a grave dug for me?" He laughed. "You don't." I got chills and a bunch of photos, and then we left for our next destination. Dale forgot his camera on a tombstone, so we had to go back at night. It was creepy, but we obviously lived to tell about it. Joe asks readers to please leave him alone: It gets tiresome chasing all the curiosity seekers away night after night.

By the way, we never heard from Eric Tapout again. But on another note, years later we did spot the "Ghost Deer" of Buckout Road up in Seneca Falls on protected land. Obviously, they left the area for a more low-rent location. Anyway, I snapped a picture of them as proof that the Indians' legend actually turns out to be true.

CHAPTER 13: EXECUTION ROCKS

When you read this chapter you will see there are many horrible tales surrounding this tiny island and its lighthouse. Unfortunately, their tour season was already over when I decided to do this chapter and so could not go out there by their tour boats or stay overnight to see the island up close and personal. So my husband and I, along with my son, Spencer, and his fiancée, Heather, decided we would take our boat and get close enough to grab a photo, without trespassing, of course—no good getting arrested just to get a photo for this book. We have owned various boats for over a decade and have never had problems with them. We were coming from Ossining and had to head south to get to Execution Rock. On the way down we were stopped for an hour by a closed bridge, Devils Bridge (Spuyten Duyvil) of all names, but we were still determined to get the photo so we journeyed on. But all of a sudden as we got closer, the out-drive gave out! We had to putt-putt-putt all the way back home and were never able to make our destination. Did we hit something in the water or was it the tortured souls of Execution Rock who have made it abundantly clear they do not want people on their island? Ironically, though, they do have a bed-and-breakfast service, so the leftover souls can't be too harsh on us humans. The owner, Craig Morrison, said, "A lot of comedians have chosen to stay overnight."

Being a comic myself, all I can say is, "They were looking for new material!" and, apparently, I got some without even getting to visit!

Finally, a few general observations: First, there are always believers and people who swear what they have seen is true. Second, how come there are never any naked ghosts? All the ghosts that haunt places always have clothes on, and they are tattered. If there is an afterlife, can't they get a better deal on clothes? Third, since I wrote the first edition, there are a lot more home videos online of the things I spoke about in these chapters. You can peruse them on YouTube and decide for yourself if it looks legit or Photoshopped. Fourth, in these chapters I've only touched on the details of these mysteries, as I was limited to the amount of words each chapter could contain. Each chapter subject alone has books and a massive amount of other information out there. My goal was to introduce you to it and pique your curiosity over whether these events and places even existed. You can go off and explore more about it on your own as you see fit. Lastly, the wonderful thing about being human is our creative mind and imagination; the world would be very boring without myths and mysteries, and everyone believing in the same thing. It's up to you as an open-minded reader to decide if you need to have tangible evidence to believe something is true. May you always be curious, and one day become a legend, at least in your own mind!

CHAPTER 1

Is That an Alligator in the Sewer?

On the cold, wintry day of February 10, 1935, a couple of teens decided to be good Samaritans by shoveling the snow around their East 123rd Street neighborhood in Harlem. They had their system down to a science. They would shovel the snow off the street and deposit it into an open manhole. One teen would act as lookout to make sure the manhole wasn't piled too deeply and the others would take turns depositing their shovelfuls of snow. It was dusk and they had been going at it for a while, so the pile was getting higher and higher.

It was sixteen-year-old Salvatore Condulucci's turn at manhole rim duty. As he signaled, his teammates would drop the blackened slush into the hole. He would clean up any snow around the rim and then they would repeat the process. All of a sudden, as he was about to give the go-ahead for the next heap to be dumped into the manhole, he noticed that the area ten feet below him looked clogged up. He held up his hands to his friends, saying, "Hey, you guys, wait a minute." He dropped to his knees to get a better look into the dark hole that led to the murky waters of the Harlem River.

As he strained to look, he noticed that the pile of snow was starting to move. He looked closer. Maybe it was melting, and the settling of the snow was causing the movement. That's when he saw it—a large black object breaking through the dirty, slush-filled heap. His eyes widened. He leaped back almost losing his balance and yelled to his friends, "Honest, it's an alligator."

Sal's two friends, Jimmy Mireno and Frank Lonzo, ran over to take a look for themselves. Jimmy nudged Frank out of the way and stuck his head in the manhole opening. He looked up and nodded in agreement. Frank, of course, wanted to look in as well to confirm with his own eyes the existence of this out-of-place reptile. Just as Frank was about to see for himself, there was a great crushing sound. More curious than scared, they stuck their heads in the hole to see what was happening. It was then they realized the poor creature's dilemma. It was lodged in the ice, thrashing about, trying to free itself from its potentially icy grave. They looked at each other and decided that they would help the alligator out.

The boys quickly ran to the Lehigh Stove and Repair Shop located at 441 East 123rd Street. Salvatore, the self-delegated leader of the group, looked around to see what was available. Since stores in New York City don't usually have a "How to Catch a Wayward Alligator Kit" on hand, they had to come up with a makeshift solution. A fan of Western movies, Salvatore figured he could shape some clothesline rope that he spotted into a lasso. They bought the clothesline and ran back to the sewer where the reptilian victim was waiting. With his friends watching, Salvatore made a slipknot and carefully lowered the rope into the darkened sewer. Not having much practice in the capturing of wayward lizards, he had to lower the rope several times to get it around the alligator's neck. After several attempts, the alligator was on the line. Salvatore yelled to his friends to grab the rope and help heave the behemoth up. The leathery creature was now struggling to get free from both the rope and the mounds of snow and ice that were heaped on him, and he was losing his strength. Slowly, with all the strength they could muster, the teens lifted the alligator out of the sewer and onto the snow-laden streets of New York City.

The animal lay there dazed. The boys looked at the gator. The gator looked at the boys. Since it was still tightly lassoed, the boys decided to let the animal have some breathing room. One of them went over to loosen the noose. Since the alligator was confused, weakened, and stunned from its ordeal, as soon as it felt slack on the rope, it opened its toothy jaws and snapped. It wasn't a vicious snap, but the snap of a tired, scared, homesick alligator that had no clue if these boys were friend or foe. Unfortunately for the creature, it found out very soon. It was not the answer it was hoping for.

The boys, who a moment before had had sympathy for the reptile, were annoyed that this ungrateful animal had startled them. With their adrenaline rushing, their caveman instincts of flight or fight kicked in. Someone shouted, "Let 'im have it!" The group of gator avengers turned savage, bashing the weakened creature on the head with their shovels. The gator fought back but was too tired to put up a real fight. Within moments it lay there, dead on its snowy grave.

With hearts racing, the boys dropped their weapons and looked at each other. They had killed the beast that they had struggled to rescue moments before. Brushing those feelings aside, they decided to drag their trophy gator to the store where only minutes before they had bought the life-saving rope. Intrigued by this unusual catch, the owner of the Lehigh Stove and Repair Shop helped the boys weigh and measure all 8 feet and 125 pounds of the dead gator. (A gator of this length would typically weigh about 300 pounds.)

As with most unusual events, word quickly spread in the neighborhood and everyone came out to have a gander at the leathery beast. Speculation began as to where this alligator could have escaped from. Since there were no local pet shops or people who claimed to have a pet alligator living in their bathtub, these possibilities were ruled out. There were no reports of missing alligators from the zoo. The neighborhood consensus was that the gator had escaped from a passing steamer boat that had been carrying it from the Everglades. Somehow it fell overboard and found itself in cold waters, so it swam for shore. Disoriented, it found an opening to the sewer system through one of its conduits and ducked in there for cover, probably trying to use the tunnel as a way home. However, the gator couldn't have gone far because it had to work its way through the melting snow in the system. Slowly starving and freezing to death, it lay under the only bit of sunlight it could find, beneath the open manhole where the boys had originally spotted it.

At 9 p.m., after a few hours of gazing at the dead gator, the boys' mothers rounded up the crew and took them home. At that point, someone called the police. The New York City police, being used to unusual things, did not rush over. After all, the alligator was already dead, and there was no law on the books that could be applied to dead alligators, escaped alligators, or killers of alligators if they didn't know who the beast in question belonged to. The store owner was left to handle the creature as he wished.

He decided to call the sanitation department, which incinerated the carcass at Barren Island. Shortly after, the story appeared in the *New York Times.* Statements were taken from the boys, the store owner, and some local eyewitnesses, but since the body had already been disposed of, some surmised that the event could have been the collective imagination of a neighborhood looking for attention.

Although this Harlem tale was the first detailed story of alligators in the sewers of New York, it was not the first sighting ever reported. On July 18, 1831, the *Planet*, a local newspaper in Union Village, New York, made reference to an alligator spotting, reporting, "A live Alligator," it is said, "was seen on Friday in the slip between Murray's and Pine Street wharves, New York."

This whimsical statue by Tom Otterness captures the spirit of one of New York's most mysterious sewer dwellers. If you look closely, you can see the words NYC SEWER written on the cover. The statue is cleverly located in the subway station at the corner of the 8th Avenue and 14th Street station. It is tucked under the staircase that leads down from the A train, on the L train platform.
PHOTO COURTESY OF SPENCER PATTERSON

The idea that alligators lived in the New York City sewers first gained credence, however, when a rash of reported sightings (the Harlem story was one) occurred during the 1930s. Since then, for nearly ninety years, alligators have been said to thrive in the dark recesses of the Big Apple sewer system. With over 6,500 miles of sewer lines in the city, which range in size from six-inch pipes to giant shells, from brick sewers circa 1840 to concrete structures, it is possible that if alligators are there, they can easily move about without being seen on a daily basis.

If this legend is true, how exactly did all these alligators come to live in the sewers in the first place? The most common explanation is that the snowbirds in New York were ignoring state law and returning from their tropical vacations with small alligators as exotic pets for their children. When the gators got too big, their owners would flush them down the toilet and the gators would end up in the sewers. (It seems a bit far-fetched that a large alligator would fit down a toilet. It's more likely the owners would avoid the middleman by putting the alligators directly into the sewers themselves.)

Some of the alligators were said to have survived the journey from toilet to sewer, managing to live in the dank atmosphere by dining on rats and garbage. These alligators then reproduced, and because they were in the dark, many of their offspring adapted and mutated into albinos. Colonies of the albino alligators were supposedly living in the sewers and menacing sewer workers.

Indeed the story grew legs when a credible eyewitness report came in from Teddy May, a superintendent of the New York City sewers. May claimed that while he worked in the sewers in the

1930s he heard reports from his inspectors that there were alligators in the sewers. He refused to believe it and thought instead the men were sneaking booze on the job. So he hired spies to watch his inspectors to see if they were intoxicated and fabricating these wild tales. Reports came back that the men were sober and were indeed dealing with narrow escapes from the alligators. Still not convinced, May decided to go down into the sewers himself and put an end to these rumors. Instead he returned a few hours later, visibly shaken, saying that two-foot-long alligators were indeed alive and thriving in colonies. He further explained that they were not living in the main fast-water sewer lines but in the smaller, slower-moving water lines in the backwash of the city. He believed they were not dumped down toilets but instead down storm drains where they made their way into the sewers.

After his shocking discovery, he made it his mission to supervise the eradication of the reptiles. To do this he used rat poison or corralled the alligators toward the larger pipes with fast-moving water so they could be swept out to sea or drown. According to May, other, more unorthodox methods were also used. Men were stationed outside the large pipes, and when gators exited, they were shot to ensure they wouldn't lurk in the waters and make their way back in. Others of the subterranean freeloaders were hunted by inspectors in the tunnel system with .22 caliber guns and rifles and shot on sight.

While this extermination was going on, stories of alligator sightings continued to appear in newspapers, which reinforced the idea of the sewer-dwellers in people's minds. There was often just enough truth in the stories to perpetuate the legend. For example, the *New York Times* reported on June 30, 1932, that there was a "swarm" of alligators spotted near the Bronx River. Upon further investigation, it turned out that a child had found one dead, three-foot alligator. Other reports surfaced on March 7, 1935, when a live, three-foot alligator was rounded up in Northern Yonkers, and soon after that a dead, six-foot reptile was found at Grass Sprain. By 1937 May announced that he and his workers had rid the sewers of the gators. But apparently the creatures did not get the memo. While they might have been out of the sewers, according to May, they apparently were not easily intimidated and were still infesting the New York area.

On May 31, 1937, a sober East River barge captain working at Pier 9 said he spotted a four-foot gator swimming toward him from the Brooklyn shore. Maybe it was a gator that had escaped the guns of May's men in the sewers or, as theorized at the time, another escapee from the boats coming in from the Everglades. No one knew for sure. Why the alligators would hitch rides on these boats and how they escaped if they were unwilling passengers in transit in the first place are still mysteries. Either way the stories continued to surface, as did the reptiles. However, not all of the alligators wanted to reside in Manhattan. On June 6, 1937, one alligator apparently decided to try out the transit system. This adventurous, two-foot gator was caught by an unruffled New Yorker at the Brooklyn Museum subway station, and another five alligators were captured in 1938 in New Rochelle.

The urban legend of the sewer-dwelling alligators forever became a standardized part of New York culture in the 1960s when two popular books came out around the same time: *The World*

Beneath the City by Robert Daley (1959), in which the author interviews Teddy May and documents his account, and a 1963 novel by Thomas Pynchon, *V*, in which the author talks about the "cute little pet alligators purchased as Florida souvenirs that eventually were discarded down toilets." Pynchon's book, which was nominated for a National Book Award, details the alligator hunts in the sewers, and how big, blind albino gators lurked there in the dark shadows. By this time, New Yorkers accepted the fact that they had nonpaying Floridian residents in their midst.

As the years went on, other sightings were reported, but skeptics started to refute the stories. The *New York Times* published an article dated May 19, 1982, in which John T. Flaherty, the chief of design at the New York City Bureau of Sewers, said the alligators were all a myth. (By now Teddy May was retired.) Flaherty claimed, "There is not enough space, there is not enough food and the torrents of water that run through the sewers during a heavy rain would drown even an alligator." He further reasoned that the clear proof of the absence of alligators was "that not a single union official has ever advanced alligator infestation as a reason for a pay increase for sewer workers." Based on this reasoning, Flaherty debunked it all as a "myth." He never personally checked, however.

As is common with any good legend, especially one that is founded on some truth, there are experts on both sides of the fence. Some say alligators could not exist in the sewers because of lack of sunlight; others say there is enough of a food supply and they could exist, especially if the alligators venture out of the sewers in the day for sunlight and then back to the dark tunnels at night to sleep. In an attempt to settle this dispute, the television show *Monster*

Quest set out to find the answer. What the investigators found was surprising. They discovered that various heat sources keep the sewer environment warm enough for alligators to survive. There is enough of a food supply to live on and there is enough material available that alligators could make nests. The sewers could indeed be an "ideal habitat." Although the television crew was unsuccessful in spotting a gator during their filming and research, they did find another reptile, a salamander, residing there. A salamander, they reasoned, would be just as unlikely to take up residence in the sewers as its more famous relatives.

Meanwhile, while the camera-shy sewer alligators stayed out of the *Monster Quest* spotlight, another alligator came into the limelight around the same time. In August of 1982, a twenty-six-inch gator was spotted sunning in a Westchester reservoir by several residents. Maybe it was a celebrity gator, taking in the local sun.

A few years later, not to be outdone, another Gotham gator turned up in Kissena Park in Queens in July of 1997, according to the *New York Times*. This four-footer was thought to be "just an illegal pet alligator," not a sewer dweller and was promptly shipped back to Jacksonville, Florida.

Of course, as they say in real estate, location, location, location is everything, and one gator found its way to prime property. According to the Associated Press, on June 16, 2001, a twenty-four-inch gator was spotted in Harlem Meer Lake, which is in the northeastern section of Central Park. Over two dozen people, including some park employees and an off-duty policeman, spotted the creature. More police rushed to the scene. Within minutes they roped off the area and began searching for the leathery intruder who lurked in the park's public waters. But the creature's stealth abilities allowed it to elude its pursuers.

For days the Associated Press did follow-up stories on the hunt, but the gator was laying low. Several government officials were called in as the public grew uneasy about this uncaptured beast. One official, Charles Sturcken, New York City's chief of the Environmental Protection Agency, suggested to the press that when they caught the gator it should be returned to its "natural habitat," the sewer. He was only partially joking. He reasoned that the New York City winter and the water temperature of Central Park lake would be too cold for it to survive outdoors and that the "sewer system is much warmer and is the city's answer to the natural swamp, with 6,000 miles of tunnels and a billion gallons of water, replenished every day."

Sturcken's statement to the press once again opened the decades-long debate. Herpetologists argued that the pollution alone in the sewer system would kill any living thing. Frank Indiviglio, a reptile specialist at the Staten Island Zoo, said that "the sewers are too polluted, too cold and there is not enough sunlight" for alligators to survive. But the believers and nonbelievers could argue all they wanted, the bottom line was there was an uncaptured alligator right there for the world to see in the middle of New York City.

The city was on edge for five days while the famed Central Park Gator, now identified as a South American spectacled caiman and nicknamed "Damon the Caiman" by Parks Commissioner Henry Stern, was still on the loose. Mike and Tina Bailey, Florida-based husband-and-wife alligator wranglers, were flown in to capture the creature. During their first attempt at capture, the skilled team realized that the creature was hiding from the bright spotlights of the camera crews that waited around the lake. The wranglers asked for the lights to be brought down and in minutes, Tina Bailey spotted Damon the Caiman and quickly scooped him up "like a loaf of bread," just a few feet from a surprised cameraman. The crowd cheered as the Central Park waters were safe again.

There was a brief "custody battle" between Florida and New York for two-year-old Damon, but in the end, New York City once again had an alligator in its midst. Publicists in Florida had been ready to send out press releases that the gator was coming home, but the slick New York City officials had made the wrangler team sign a paper before they were allowed to capture the creature, which stated that the gator would be the property of New York City and would be housed in the Central Park Zoo. Charles Sturcken explained "that alligators are reptiles of honor" in New York City, and while the gator's rightful home was underneath the Big Apple, it would probably be just as "happy in the zoo."

But the alligator stories don't end there. In November 2006, a two-foot-long caiman was captured outside an apartment building in Brooklyn. It hissed and snapped at the police on being taken into custody: Apparently even reptiles adopt the New York attitude.

With all these eyewitness accounts and news stories, it appears that the tales of alligators in the sewers of New York are indeed based in truth. And to honor this, since 2010 Michael Miscione, the official Manhattan borough historian, has been observing February 9 as "Alligators in the Sewers Day"—an unofficial holiday to honor discarded pets or escaped beasts that have grown large in the belly of our streets. Mr. Miscione also points out that currently the US Postal Service has regulation 526.6 stipulating that alligators "not exceeding 20 inches in length may be shipped through the mail"! (Small ones have even been shipped in a ramen noodle package!) Although as a side note, it is illegal to own an alligator now as a pet in New York City, but as late as July 26, 2017, an alligator was spotted in Upstate New York by kayakers and verified by the New York State Department of Environmental Conservation. So while these resilient reptiles have moved on to greener pastures, that doesn't stop people from honoring their NYC legend. In February 2017, an alligator trophy was awarded by Kevin Walsh, the creator of the Forgotten New York website, to people up on their alligator trivia. After all, you never know when this may be a question on "Who Wants to Be a Millionaire"!

Bottom line, while some of the stories may have been exaggerated as to the size and number of gators seen in one encounter, and there has never been an actual albino gator found or sighted in the sewers, there is much more evidence to prove that alligators existed in New York City and the surrounding areas than not. Whether they retreated at night to the sewers to sleep is unknown, but they obviously were living somewhere, and since a gator can live as long as fifty years, the sewer seems just as good a place as any for them to take up residence. If you ever find yourself for some bizarre reason in the New York City sewer system, beware; you don't know what creepy reptile may still be lurking there, waiting for its next press appearance or a tender bite to eat.

CHAPTER 2

Famous Ghosts of the Dakota

Many places in New York are said to be haunted by ghosts of a bygone era. Often ghosts of children in old-fashioned clothes are seen playing in courtyards and running down hallways. If there has been foul play in a particular area or residence, then perhaps a ghost has stayed to search for and pay justice to the perpetrator. Usually these spirits are not of the celebrity kind. There is one building in Manhattan, however, that is said to have famous ghosts haunting its luxury facilities. Located at 1 West 72nd Street in Manhattan, that building is the Dakota.

When Edward C. Clark, co-founder of the Singer Sewing Machine Company, dreamed of building housing far north of all the activity in New York City, he was laughed at. He paid five million dollars to investment banker Jacob Schiff for a plot of farmland. People nicknamed his place the Dakota after the Dakota Territory out west, making fun of its remote location. But Clark envisioned a luxury apartment house—one like the world had never seen. Clark hoped that a rich clientele would be attracted to the money they could save by living in one dwelling with multiple homes; people would share the cost of security and a full-service building with amenities. He hired the architectural firm of Henry Janeway Hardenbergh to make his dream come true.

From the start, people believed his building was doomed to failure. They mocked the dreamer and called his building "Clark's Folly." Unfortunately, Clark died in 1882, two years before the building was complete. But Clark was the one laughing, even if it was from heaven. When it opened its doors in 1884, the building was already fully rented, with the Steinway family of Steinway piano fame as one of its first residents. The *New York Times* billed the Dakota as "one of the most perfect apartment houses in the world." It was the first of its kind, a luxury apartment building complete with a playroom, gymnasium, tennis courts, and private croquet lawns. There were sixty-five residential apartments ranging from a mere four rooms to a lavish twenty rooms. The outside of the building had a North German Renaissance appeal, complete with finials, decorative balconies, balustrades, and a pitched copper-slate roof with ornate railings. Being infatuated with appearance, but still wanting safety, the architects purposely avoided putting fire escapes in because they didn't like the look, so instead they slathered mud from Central Park between the layers of brick flooring to both fireproof and soundproof the building.

The building was arranged around a courtyard square; the entrance into the courtyard was an arched passage large enough that a horse-drawn carriage could easily drive through. Carriages could then drop off their passengers in this sheltered area; if there was inclement weather, the occupants wouldn't be inconvenienced like other mere mortals. And there was always a white gloved doorman posted twenty-four hours a day to welcome all who entered.

The outside of the building was very ornate, and some found it eerie, so a third nickname was given to it, the "Dracula." As a final touch, a figure of a Dakota Indian was placed above the single entranceway to keep a watchful eye over its special residents.

The interior of the building was laid out in a French style popular during its construction. One unique and novel feature of the Dakota was that the main rooms such as the master bedrooms faced the street, while the dining rooms and kitchens faced the courtyard. This allowed the apartments to get air circulation from two sides. Other apartment buildings at the time had windows on only one side. The Dakota also featured fourteen-foot-high ceilings that allowed for grand chandeliers and a feeling of openness. The floors were inlaid with mahogany, oak, and cherry wood, giving it a lavish touch. Of course, the owner, Clark, saved the best for himself; some of his floors were inlaid with sterling silver. Another bonus feature was that no two apartments were alike; everyone would get a unique living space to occupy.

To further cater to upscale clients, there was a large common dining hall downstairs; residents could choose to dine there or have their meals sent up by dumbwaiter. The building also had its own central heating, as well as an in-house plant for electricity. With all this luxury, the Dakota was in instant success.

But who could afford these Upper West Side apartments and their huge price tag? Early on members of high society and, later, Hollywood celebrities flocked to the building en masse.

Over the years a list of the residents of the Dakota would read like a Who's Who of Hollywood and society's rich and famous. Residents at one time or another included Lauren Bacall (who had her nine-room apartment for fifty-three years, and it sold for $23.5 million), Leonard Bernstein, Connie Chung and husband Maury

Povich, Judy Garland, Boris Karloff, Neil Sedaka, Roberta Flack, John Madden, Gilda Radner, Steve Guttenberg, Judy Holiday, playwright William Inge, film critic Rex Reed, interior decorator Syrie Maugham, Rosemary Clooney, Jack Palance, Lillian Gish, and sportsman F. Ambrose Clark, who was also the grandson of the famed builder himself.

The building had zero vacancies from 1884 to 1929! Contrary to popular belief, though, being famous or involved in the entertainment industry was not a surefire way to gain approval from the co-op board. Some celebrities did get turned down. For example, in 1970 Gene Simmons of Kiss wanted an apartment but was turned down by the board, and he wasn't even in his full makeup and stage garb at the time! Others who have been turned down over the years were Melanie Griffith, Antonio Banderas, Cher, Madonna, Carly Simon, Alex Rodriguez, Judd Apatow, and Tea Leoni.

The building gained even more fame when its beautiful architecture and luxury made it a perfect candidate for addition to the National Register of Historic Places. It was added to the prestigious list in 1972. Four years later, it was declared a historic landmark. This made the building even more desirable to the jet-set crowd. Once again, not all celebrities got in. Billy Joel put in a request to live in the building on September 25, 1977, but, as in the case of the Kiss bassist, he was given thumbs down by the board.

But the Dakota is most associated with one entertainer in particular, John Lennon. In 1973, shortly after his wife died, actor, former marine, and longtime civil rights activist Robert Ryan sublet his apartment, number 72, to Lennon and his wife, Yoko Ono. Upon moving in, Lennon and Ono hired a psychic to read the spiritual energy of the apartment. Supposedly, through the psychic, they contacted the deceased Mrs. Ryan. When Ryan himself died, his estate sold the apartment to them. At first some of the other conservative residents did not want Lennon moving in, but eventually, outside of a few pranks and their artsy clothing fashions, Lennon and Ono fit in.

They lived there in peace. Lennon had long since left his original claim to fame as a member of the iconic British group, The Beatles, and was a star on his own. He went on to produce hit songs like "Give Peace a Chance" and "Imagine." He retired from 1976 to 1980, but then the music bug hit him again and he came out of retirement, producing *Double Fantasy,* an album that won a 1981 Grammy for Album of the Year. Yes, he and Ono were very happy.

Then came that tragic day—a day that Lennon had predicted, ironically, many years earlier. While still with The Beatles, Lennon was asked during a radio interview how he thought he would die. He laughed, "I'll probably be popped off by some loony." That loony happened to be Mark David Chapman. The crazed twenty-five-year-old was a Lennon fan turned stalker.

At 5 p.m. on December 8, 1980, Lennon and Ono left the Dakota for a recording session at the Record Plant Studio. As they walked toward their limo, Chapman, who had been hanging around the Dakota all day to get an autograph, went up to the limo, shook hands with Lennon, and then got him to sign a copy of his *Double Fantasy* album. A photographer happened to be there at the time and took a photo of Chapman getting it signed. Chapman then stayed around until they returned.

At 10:49 p.m. Lennon and Ono got out of their limousine and walked toward the entranceway of the Dakota, going right past Chapman who was still loitering on their street. Without warning, Chapman fired five shots from his .38 special into Lennon's back. Four shots hit Lennon's back and shoulders, but one fatal bullet pierced Lennon's aorta. Lennon stumbled into the building and yelled, "I'm shot!" Ono screamed for help. Police were on the scene in minutes, and seeing that he was severely wounded, put him in the police car and rushed him to St. Luke's Roosevelt Hospital Center. Lennon was pronounced dead at 11:07 p.m.

Ironically, Lennon had said earlier that week on an RKO radio interview that he felt safe walking anywhere in New York. Yet somewhere in the back of his mind he knew how his death would occur. Lennon had a fascination with numerology and besides his flippant remark on the radio during his days as a Beatle, he had very vivid premonitions of his own sudden death by gunshot.

When the news hit the media, two fans committed suicide. Hundreds gathered outside the building holding candles and flowers and singing "Imagine" and "Give Peace a Chance." As for Chapman, he did not attempt to run or hide. He stood there next to the smoking gun, reading a copy of *The Catcher in the Rye,* the book that he said would explain his perspective on why he had killed Lennon. The police arrested him outside the Dakota. He pleaded guilty, was charged with second-degree murder, and sentenced to twenty years to life at Attica State Prison in New York. He was moved to Wende Correctional facility in Erie County in May of 2012, and remains in protective custody in that facility. Some say

A front view of the most haunted luxury building in New York City, the Dakota, located at 1 West 72nd Street in Manhattan. It is home to many celebrities, dead and alive. The archway entrance is where Beatle John Lennon was assassinated on December 8, 1980.

his motive was instant notoriety, others say that, being a devout Christian, he took offense that Lennon once said that The Beatles were "more popular than Jesus." Because of Yoko Ono's objection, he has been denied parole six times. Since his incarceration, he has been denied parole a total of ten times, the latest in 2018. His eleventh parole hearing is scheduled for August 2020.

To pay their respects to Lennon, the city council designated a plot of land from 71st Street to 74th as Strawberry Fields, the name of one of The Beatles' songs. Every year on the anniversary of Lennon's death, there is a pilgrimage to Strawberry Fields led by Ono in homage to her late husband. Ono still lives in the Dakota as of this writing.

But although John's body left the world suddenly, his spirit has not been as fast to depart. Many supermarket tabloid articles and books have contained detailed accounts of spiritual encounters with the great musical one. The first ghostly sighting of Lennon was reported in 1983 by Joey Harrow and Amanda Moores, who claimed to have spotted Lennon standing at the entrance to the building surrounded by an "ominous light." Moores said she was going to walk up to him, but he didn't look like he wanted a human encounter, so she decided to leave him alone. (Which is a rather calm reaction to seeing a ghost, even if it is John Lennon.) Other sightings that have been reported to the media usually describe Lennon's ghost crossing from the 72nd Street entrance to the Dakota, where he was assassinated, to the "Imagine" mosaic at Strawberry Fields across Central Park West. His spirit, however, doesn't just walk; it flashes a peace sign before vanishing. His playful spirit is also said to have waved to doormen at nearby buildings, to have hummed "Give Peace a Chance" to a nearby hotdog vendor, and to have been seen popping its head out of a basement window in the Dakota, where at one point he had a studio. Others claim to have seen Lennon's ghostly spirit in his apartment building, usually around the undertaker's gate.

Another story has it that during a séance, the ghost of Lennon was contacted and it revealed that it has been in contact with the Ryans on the other side. Lennon's ghost is also said to have verified that people are not imagining things, that his sprit does "visit" the Dakota on occasion, and that spiritual activity confirming this is not that hard to detect.

One reporter, Charles Adams, spoke to the guards at the Dakota to get their take on the situation. The security guards are tight lipped as to whether the Lennon ghost story is true or not. One guard, who preferred to remain nameless, said that he "doesn't believe in ghosts." But when pressed, he did admit that there have been numerous ghost stories in the place over the years and many have come from reliable tenants.

But Yoko Ono herself told about the most famous ghost sighting of Lennon. According to one *New York Post*'s Page Six posting, Yoko said she saw her husband sitting at the piano in their apartment and he turned to her and said, "Don't be afraid. I am still with you." then vanished.

The odd thing is, prior to Lennon's own death he claimed to have seen a "Crying Lady" walking the halls of the building. Some believe that "Crying Lady" was the spirit of Elise Vesley, a woman who was into the paranormal herself and was said to claim to have psychokinetic powers (she could move large objects with her mind). She also happened to be the "lady managerette" of the Dakota building from the 1930s to 1950s. She was said to be whimsical with her screening of prospective tenants and favor those into Vendantism (an Eastern religious cult), which she was very involved in. She was also extremely fond of children since her young son was killed by a truck in front of the Dakota, and she was said to be "peculiar" ever since. Some claim she roams the building protecting the children spirits that roam the halls.

So who are these other ghosts that don't want to leave the premises? Apparently, the Hollywood King of Horror, Boris Karloff, still haunts the building as well. He is said to roam the halls, which would be a very fitting role for Karloff. Since he scared people with his screen image while he was alive, why not keep shocking them after his death? Not to be outdone, celebrity resident Judy Garland, who lived in apartment 77 and is famous for her portrayal of Dorothy in *The Wizard of Oz,* apparently did not go somewhere over the rainbow after her death. She, too, lingers on in the Dakota.

Along with celebrity ghosts, there is also a supporting cast of ghostly residents. A ten-year-old boy dressed in 1900s garb is often seen by workers. A little long-haired blonde girl, who also dresses in turn-of-the-century clothes, specifically a yellow taffeta dress that matches her hair, white stockings, and black leather shoes with silver buckles, likes to bounce her ball in the hallway and has been seen on numerous occasions. Many have reported her saying, "Today's my birthday." Then she smiles and disappears. Others say they see children in the lobby; the children then walk off into a closet and disappear. These ghosts are believed to have taken up residence during the time of the building's beginnings, from 1881 to 1884.

According to witnesses, these ghosts not only make their presence known visually, but they emit an odor as well. It has been reported that the phantoms are often accompanied by a stale smell. Who knows, maybe there's no laundry on the spirit side, and, let's face it, these kids, even though they are in ghostly form, are pretty old. (And old things do tend to smell musty.) There is also a little girl who smiles and holds out a red rose, then disappears. All of the ghosts seem to have free rein in the building; on the third floor, tenants report hearing footsteps, and rugs and chairs seem to move about of their own free will.

But it doesn't end there. What place haunted with resident ghosts would be complete without a haunted basement as well? And who better to haunt that area than the man who dreamed up the Dakota in the first place, Edward Cabot Clark. Yes, the bearded and wig-wearing short Mr. Clark with his wire-framed glasses dons a frock coat and high hat and has been spotted by many an electrician and porter in the basement. According to the website www .the13thfloor.tv, the first basement encounter was by an electrician named John Paynter in the late 1930s. He was fixing the wiring in the basement and replacing some circuitry, when Clark angrily stared at him for what seemed like an eternity, and then in a huff, Clark pulled off his hairpiece and shook it in Paynter's face before disappearing. This happened four more times to Paynter while working in the basement. Some think Clark, who died before his dream building was finished, was upset with how the electrical system was set up, so who better to take out his frustrations on than the electrician, Paynter.

Other ghostly shenanigans in the basement include what seems like a celebrity tantrum by one of the most famous set designers of the Golden Age of Broadway, Jo Mielziner. Jo died in a cab outside the Dakota in 1976. He was not only a resident of the Dakota for years, but also designed the updated elevators in the building. Shortly after his death, workers in the basement reported bags of garbage flying around the basement. Of course, some tenants scoffed at all this talk of ghostly apparitions, but they quickly changed their tune when one porter wanting an eyewitness called tenant Wilbur Ross into the basement. They witnessed a metal bar fly twenty feet off the wall and land violently by their feet. (That's one sure way to turn non-believers into believers and also make sure they never do laundry in the basement again!)

While all these spirits tend to be relatively harmless and at most some have temper tantrums, one presence seems to be downright evil, and therefore has been dubbed "The Phantom of the Dakota," aka "The Mad Slasher." This spirit is accused of creating knife-like giant slashes in the new elevators that Mielziner designed. Tenants started to notice the slashes in the paneled walls very high up in the elevator. Every week the management would have to have the panels replaced. At the same time, on the ninth floor random piles of shredded paper were piled up, a perfect setting for an "accidental" fire to start. The residents were beginning to get nervous and suspicious of each other, thinking someone was out to cause harm to either the people themselves or the building in general. It came to a head when a random paint can fell from the roof in the courtyard, barely missing a tenant. Things were getting way out of hand. Was it an angry ghost or fellow upset tenant? A secret spy club was set up and took shifts watching whomever came into the building. Not much was found except who was cheating on whom. However, the Slasher and his piles of paper disappeared, never to leave his mark again. Some say it was cranky Mr. Clark, once again upset that his dream building had been altered.

Like mentioned previously, not all the encounters happened in the public areas of the Dakota. Frederick and Suzanne Weinstein were unlucky enough to have some ghostly spirits take up residence in their apartment. Those unwelcomed ghosts particularly did not like Mr. Weinstein. Frederick would get shoved by some unseen force on multiple occasions, and constantly get injured by either a chair or a rug being pulled out from underneath him. Frederick would see lights flicker and hear footsteps pacing back and forth in the dining room. One time after playing a Ouija board–type game with his kids that involved letters on separate tiles (although why would you tempt fate with this?), the letters I-C-U appeared in his coat pocket the next day. Mischievous kids or angry ghost? Who's to say?

To add further to the eeriness of the building, the 1968 horror film *Rosemary's Baby* was filmed around the exterior of the Dakota. (Filming is not permitted in the actual building.) In the film the building was renamed The Bramford, but all astute movie fans know it was the Dakota. According to the cast and crew, the building was both creepy and intriguing to shoot around.

But there's more. The Dakota has managed to work its way numerous times into pop culture. In the popular book series "The

Baby-Sitters Club," one of the minor characters lives in the Dakota. The jam band O.A.R. wrote a song titled "Dakota" about Lennon's murder, and Tim Curry mentions the Dakota in his songs "I Do the Rock" and "20 Years in the Dakota."

Some people find it intriguing to live in a co-op building with celebrities and mysterious hauntings, while others want out and would rather have flesh and bone tenants only. As of 2016, seven apartments, including singer Roberta Flack's pad, were on the market...the asking price is a mere $7.5 million. One particular ten-room apartment, apartment 26, has been on and off the market for over eight years! Who knows—maybe it has an unwelcomed occupant who is not paying his ghostly portion of rent.

Either way, the luxurious Dakota has come a long way since its often ridiculed inception—from its majestic rise into the history books thanks to its famous tenants, to creepy onscreen appearances in horror flicks, to its landmark status, it has become a mysterious legend worldwide and in the spiritual world beyond.

CHAPTER 3

The Montauk Project

On August 12, 1943, a Navy destroyer ship named the USS *Eldridge,* based at the Philadelphia Naval Yard, was the target of an experiment known as the Rainbow Project.

The goal of this experiment was to bombard the *Eldridge* with electromagnetic energy to render its radar invisible (or cloaked), using Einstein's "Unified Field Theory." This was one of the first attempts at stealth technology and the hope was that it would put an end to World War II. A test run on an empty ship in July 1940 was successful, so the project was given unlimited funding. On the appointed day of the "real" experiment, the USS *Eldridge* had thirty-three volunteer crewmen on deck. Dr. John Eric Von Neumann, a brilliant mathematician, was in charge. (Famed inventor Nicola Tesla had initially been on the project but resigned in March 1942, due to his strong belief that an experiment with live subjects would be too risky.) Von Neumann himself said he needed more time to work out some kinks, but the Navy said he was out of time.

The command was given by the Naval brass to commence. The switch was pulled, and slowly, the generators were activated. The electromagnetic field began to take hold of the ship. Watching both ship and radar, officials were amazed when the ship slowly disappeared off of the screen. The experiment was a success. But within minutes, something went terribly wrong. A bright blue flash of light shone from the actual ship and it disappeared. The experimenters tried to make contact, but all radio communication was dead. The *Eldridge* was gone without a trace. Eyewitnesses in two states confirmed that the ship reappeared miles away in Norfolk, Virginia, and then three hours later, reappeared in the Philadelphia port with a broken mast.

At first everyone breathed a sigh of relief. The ship was back, and the stealth experiment was successful. However, they soon realized that things were not okay. In the re-materialization process, the energy and matter of people and objects had gotten fused. According to one eyewitness, Carlos Miguel Allende, a sailor who was watching the test from on board the SS *Furuseth,* "Some of the men caught fire, went mad, and—the most bizarre of all, some were embedded halfway into the deck of the ship."

The Navy held a four-day emergency meeting to decide what to do. They decided on another test run without a crew. This time, on October 28, 1943, the ship disappeared for twenty minutes, but much of the equipment was missing when it rematerialized. The Navy pulled the funding on the project.

The Rainbow Project became informally known as the Philadelphia Experiment. Since the military was still looking for superior weapons, the Philadelphia Experiment's funding was redirected into the secret Manhattan Project to develop the nuclear bombs that would ultimately end the war with Japan.

The story of the ship's disappearance was made into two movies: *The Philadelphia Experiment* (1984) and its sequel, *Philadelphia Experiment II* (1993), both based on the account above.

Most people have heard about the Philadelphia Experiment. Some say it was an elaborate hoax or legend. Some members of the USS *Eldridge* crew swear that they were on board that day and the USS *Eldridge* was not commissioned until August 27, 1943. It remained in port in New York City until September 1943. Although proponents of the story claim that the ship's logs of that date might have been falsified—and while some documents marked "classified" have appeared on the website del73.com, where personal handwritten letters from crewman, in particular Carl M. Allen, complete with sailors' ID numbers, are there in detail to examine—no one seems to be able to get conclusive evidence from tight-lipped agencies.

Still others, like Marshall Barnes, a special civilian investigator and expert on the Philadelphia Project, who appeared on the TV show *The Unexplained,* suggest that if the event did occur, there was a logical explanation. The physical ship just "seemed to disappear" with "the use of an intense electromagnetic field that would create a mirage effect of invisibility by refracting light."

But many believe that the Philadelphia Experiment was the beginning of years of secretive military and government development of the advanced stealth technology we have today. Successful technological advances come out of numerous bouts of trial and error, and the military can't announce what it's doing lest information falls into enemy hands, hence the cover-up of events, lost documents, and denials of those involved.

Supposedly the failed experiment was not the end of the Philadelphia Project. The lesser-known Montauk Project is said to have stemmed directly from those scientists who wanted to advance the technology they had learned from the USS *Eldridge* and take it a step further.

After the defunding of the Philadelphia Project, Von Neumann was reassigned to work on the atomic bomb project at Los Alamos until 1947. That same year, he was supposedly asked by the government to assist in the examination of a crashed UFO in Aztec, New Mexico (where, supposedly, sixteen small dead humanoid bodies were recovered with their undamaged seamless craft), and garner what he could from its technology.

Meanwhile, it became known that the Germans had been working on time travel since 1945 and had made significant advancement. The Phoenix Project, another secret endeavor that began in the late 1940s, was researching weather control. Experiments of the same sort were also being done in Russia. US military personnel and scientists who worked on the Philadelphia Project worried that they were losing their technological edge. The surviving researchers, consisting of Navy brass, CIA doctors, scientists, and fugitive Nazi engineers, met during 1952–1953 to continue their earlier work on electromagnetic shielding. They also wanted to use the magnetic field for mind manipulation. They asked Von Neumann if he'd take another look at the project and he agreed.

The new group created a proposal and presented it to the US Congress, stating that they could create a powerful new weapon that would alter people's minds. Congress rejected it as too dangerous and refused to fund it. Determined to get this project underway, the group revamped the proposal and presented it to the US Department of Defense. In this new proposal, they said that they could develop a weapon that would drive the enemy insane, eliciting in them the symptoms of psychotic disorders and schizophrenia using various radio frequencies. The Department of Defense approved it, which enabled the group to bypass the need for congressional approval.

The new work became an extension of the Phoenix Project. The purpose of the new entity was to conduct experiments in electronic mind surveillance (aka remote viewing), time travel, weather control, stealth technology, the creation of black holes, and psychotronics (the study of mass mind control of distinct populations of animals and people using the relationship between matter, energy, and consciousness). The ultimate purpose was to develop advanced weapons and psychological warfare. With the Defense Department's approval, all the group needed to do was get two things in place: a huge amount of funding and a secure, remote location for their experiments.

The initial operation was set up at Brookhaven National Laboratory (BNL) on Long Island. Von Neumann and Jack Pruett, who was the metaphysical director and worked for the Air Force, headed the project. It was also supervised and run by the Navy and Air Force. Many of the civilians and scientists who worked there were ex-Nazis who had come from Germany before and after the war. During the first few years, Von Neumann developed high-speed computers that were used for military and scientific research and were later said to be used in the mind-control experiments. Stealth technology also came out of these labs. But as they continued to explore radio frequencies and how these affected the mind, the scientists realized they needed a radar dish. If they built one on top of the Brookhaven lab, it would attract public attention.

They found an ideal location nearby, an old Air Force base that was "officially" decommissioned in 1969 because modern satellite technology made its 70-ton, 120-foot-wide AN/FPS-35 SAGE (Semi-Automatic Ground Environment) radar technology system obsolete. The base, known as the Montauk Air Force Station, was

The 1958 AN/FPS-35 SAGE (Semi-Automatic Ground Environment) radar installed at the Montauk Air Force Base, located at what is now Camp Hero on the tip of Montauk, Long Island, was supposedly used for mind experiments. Notice that the radar is still off-limits, even though it is on State Park land.

located on the grounds of Old Fort Hero on the easternmost tip of Long Island in a town called Montauk. In its heyday, the base had been a well-kept secret. First constructed in the 1930s to defend the coast from Hitler's U-boats, the base had been disguised as an innocent New England fishing village, with a gymnasium masquerading as a church and steeple and concrete gun emplacements with fake painted windows.

At the time (mid-1960s), Montauk was not a tourist hotspot, so it was perfect because it was far away from prying eyes, yet close to New York City. It was also close to the water, which would allow equipment to be moved in and out unnoticed. The base also had exactly what they were looking for—a radar dish. More important, the "inactive outdated" radar dish worked on a frequency of 400–425 megahertz, which was within the range of 410–420 megahertz, the frequency they felt would be able to "control and influence" the human mind and behavior. At this point, the experiments became known as the Montauk Project, which was a combination of all the previous projects.

The original funding for the Montauk Project is said to have come from Nazi gold worth $10 billion. In 1944 an American troop train was known to be carrying gold bars from Nazi war spoils that were stamped with the Black Nazi Eagle. The bars showed up ten years later in Montauk. When those funds were exhausted, additional privately funded monies supposedly came from ITT and Krupp AG in Germany, Germany's largest armaments companies.

(This is not an unusual practice. There is supposedly a source known as the Black Eagle Trust Fund, a large secret stash made up of the precious metals and gems that the Nazis and Japanese plundered from the Jews and Chinese during World War II. The United States recovered these treasures and it was determined by the US Secretary of War, Henry Stimson, that they could be clandestinely used to fund various covert operations. The Black Eagle Fund is said to still exist today and was said to have also been put into effect on 9/11 when the Securities and Exchange Commission declared a national emergency for the first time in US history and invoked its emergency powers, allowing $240 billion in covert government securities to be cleared upon maturity without standard regulatory controls around identification of ownership.)

What transpired next with the Montauk project sounds like a script from a sci-fi movie. The secret construction began on a multi-level subterranean complex with the help of the National Security Agency (NSA) and the Office of Naval Intelligence (ONI). The project was under US government surveillance, with the CIA monitoring everything.

All the equipment was moved from BNL to the Air Force base during 1967–1968. By then Von Neumann was dead. To avoid suspicion, the base was "officially" decommissioned in 1969, and the land above the underground matrix was donated as a wildlife refuge, which was never opened to the public because of "environmental contamination." (What kind of refuge is that for animals?)

Meanwhile, the Montauk project was fully functional nine floors below street level. By the early 1970s the underground base was conducting mind experiments using mathematical theorems, quantum mechanics, and cutting-edge technology. When stumped, the investigators supposedly had help from extraterrestrials. (Always good to have one or two of them on staff!)

Who were the test subjects? There were rumors that some were homeless people and abducted runaways. However, the majority of the important subjects were reported to be young men with psychic sensitivity. These men were asked to participate in the mind experiments voluntarily. The project's top subject was a strong psychic man, Duncan Cameron. It is reported that Cameron and a man named Al Bielek were two sailors who had jumped off the *Eldridge* during the 1943 Philadelphia Experiment and were stuck traveling back and forth in time.

Cameron, like all the other test subjects, would participate in various experiments. The first experiment he was involved in was called "The Seeing Eye." With just a lock of a person's hair or an object a person owned, he would concentrate on the person and be able to observe as if he were inside the person's body, seeing through his or her eyes, hearing through his or her ears, or feeling through the person's hands. He had this ability no matter where that person was on Earth.

The majority of the mind experiments lasted from 1969 to 1979, and reportedly involved an estimated 300,000 test subjects, mostly male. Only 1 percent survived.

A subject would be placed about 250 feet away from an antenna. The SAGE radar would then radiate a gigawatt of power at the subject. Often the heat from the radar would destroy brain functions, create neurological damage, and scar lungs. There were few survivors, but because many of the subjects were indigent, no one came looking for them.

A teleportation portal was created that would allow researchers to travel anywhere in time or space using a D1 base time tunnel.

Visits to Mars and contact with extraterrestrials were made through this tunnel, and this is one area in which alien advice helped enhance the Montauk Project. (They were like the travel agents of this project!)

Another device aliens were supposed to have advised on was the Montauk Chair. The chair was based on 1950s technology that the German ITT company had developed. The subject would sit in a chair, which was surrounded by sensory coils that were set up in a pyramid fashion. Three sets of coils were then hooked up to three receivers that would display on the screen what the person was thinking. In essence this was a mind-reading machine, which took the electromagnetic functions of the human brain and translated them into a language that the computer could read. It worked similarly to the way human speech is carried by radio waves, except that in this case thoughts were carried by aura waves. The chair was blasted with airwaves that would then control the subject's mind.

In doing these experiments, they found Cameron, their strongest psychic, was able to focus on an object so intensely that the object would actually become visible for a moment. He could then picture any location in the world and the object would appear there. (A prototype duplicate of the Montauk Chair was given to England and put in a facility on the Thames River.)

One unwilling subject and rare survivor, a Long Island man by the name of Stewart Swerdlow, claims to have been abducted several times between the ages of thirteen and seventeen and used in the Montauk genetic experiment program. Today he is an author, lecturer, linguist medical intuitive, and clairvoyant. He talks openly about the Montauk Project and says that, as a result, his "psionic" (the practice of using the mind to induce paranormal phenomena like telepathy and telekinesis) faculties were boosted, but at the cost of emotional instability, post-traumatic stress disorder, and other issues." (Not to mention that he may have fathered a kid somewhere with an alien.)

But the experiments didn't stop with the chair. The scientists found that different frequencies would produce various results in the subjects, actually altering their mood from happy, to angry, to aggressive, to sad. They proved their theory and learned that in fact a frequency of 410–420 megahertz would jam psychic abilities and change the mood of everyone on the base.

To test this further, they used the radar to send frequencies into the town at a certain time each day. The chief of police reported a pattern of increased crime during that time. Even animals were affected and were reported coming into town en masse, sometimes crashing through windows as in a scene out of *Jumanji*.

The reports excited the scientists. They realized that if they could manipulate people and time-space reality, they were really onto a superpower war weapon. They were determined to perfect their experiments.

However, the implications of this new-found weapon frightened some at the base who felt the project was veering too far toward world domination. They felt it had to end. The opposition saw its chance on August 12, 1983. On that date, an experiment would attempt to go back exactly forty years to August 12, 1943, to reconnect with the sailors aboard the USS *Eldridge*. Since the Earth has a natural biorhythm that peaks in twenty-year cycles on

August 12, the experimenters thought it would provide a connecting link for the two experiments in hyperspace. The scientists had already manipulated and created wormholes in which a person could travel to the past and future. They decided to send Cameron through the time tunnel to find out what went wrong in 1943.

Here is where two different endings come into play. Some say arguments ensued and those who wanted to end the experiments instructed Cameron to go back in time to the USS *Eldridge* and destroy the generator, thus making the time tunnel collapse in on itself.

Another version has it that on August 12, 1983, at the appointed time, when the wormhole allowed for the USS *Eldridge* and the Montauk Project to coexist, Cameron was in the Montauk Chair. Someone leaned over and said to him, "The time is now." With that, the 1983 Cameron visualized a hairy, angry, Sasquatch-like creature nine feet tall. The raging beast destroyed the mind-harnessing equipment at the Montauk base, and the time tunnel that the scientists had kept open collapsed in on itself. Some say both events happened simultaneously.

Shortly after, the Montauk project ended. In June of 1984, Black Berets went in and removed any remaining equipment. Six months later, a convoy of cement trucks dumped cement down the elevator shafts and covered many of the underground passageways. Many people supposedly saw these trucks. Then the place was gated up and abandoned forever. Eyewitnesses who could leak information were supposedly brainwashed, relocated into the witness protection program, or debriefed and sworn to an eternal oath of secrecy.

How do we know all this? To answer that we have to back-track to 1974, when Long Island–born Preston Nichols, an electrical engineer who was a specialist in the field of electromagnetic phenomena, was working for a well-known defense contractor near Montauk. Having degrees also in parapsychology and psychology, he was given a grant to study mental telepathy and to determine whether or not it existed. It was during his experiments with psychic subjects that he noticed peculiar phenomena. Every day at the same time their psychic minds became jammed. He figured that some kind of electronic signal caused them to become nonfunctional. Using his radio equipment, he noticed that whenever there was a wave of 410–420 megahertz, his subjects were jammed. Using an antenna on the roof of his car, he tracked the signal to the Air Force base in Montauk. He found out that the airbase was still active, although the security guards denied this, telling him that the radar was being run by the FAA. Nichols knew that didn't make sense because the World War II SAGE radar was antiquated and there was no reason for the FAA to be using it. Suspicious, he started to do research, but for the next decade, found nothing substantial.

It wasn't until November of 1984 when Duncan Cameron walked into Nichols's lab that he started to put the pieces together. Cameron quickly became absorbed into the group of psychics that Nichols was working with. Slowly, he and Nichols uncovered the Montauk project's purpose. They got a lead, were told the base was abandoned, and began to search around.

Nichols got more friends involved in the search but began to fear for his life as he uncovered evidence that he had been involved in the project at one point, but had no memory of it. He was worried he might end up dead, so he gave a public talk about his findings at the US Psychotronics Association in Chicago. It caused quite a commotion, but also guaranteed he would not be silenced or killed by the government.

Since then, Nichols has become the leading authority on the Montauk Project. Determined to expose the project and its workings, he has written several books and done many radio shows and Internet interviews on the subject. He has also remembered time-traveling himself on two occasions and says that the experience felt as if he were dying and being reborn. He now claims that he was present when Cameron was in the Montauk Chair.

As for the Montauk site itself, it was opened to the public on September 18, 2002, as Camp Hero State Park, but the military still owns all the ground underneath. The radar tower has been placed on the State and National Register of Historic Places. Despite rumors, no traces of secret underground facilities have been found, although there is a hill with concrete-sealed doors on the grounds of Camp Hero.

The Montauk Project's scientific theories have influenced several films. It was the inspiration for *Total Recall:* Arnold Schwarzenegger sits in a similar alien chair before going to Mars. In the film *Eternal Sunshine of the Spotless Mind,* Jim Carrey talks about jump rooms and a seat that can take people anywhere they want to go by the power of their mind. Montauk is mentioned in the film several times and the film crew attempted to get permission to film on location at the Air Force base, but were denied. Finally, Netflix's *Stranger Things* was sold under the working title

Montauk, with the theme of the Montauk Project looping through eight of its episodes. The character Eleven goes through some of the experiments the supposed "Montauk Project" victims went through before she opens the portal to the Upside Down.

Reporters have tried to investigate the base with little success. One lead involved Enrico Chekov, a Spanish-Russian dissident who defected to America in 19 88. He told of a satellite surveillance photo captured behind the Iron Curtain during the 1970s that showed the formation of a large bubble of space-time centered on the Montauk site, which lent more support to the D1 base time travel tunnel story. A reporter from the *New York Times* got wind of Chekov's story and asked to see the photo. The day after, Chekov's Manhattan apartment was ransacked and the photo was the only thing taken. The *New York Times* reporter backed off as he investigated further and supposedly discovered that much of what had been said about the project was true.

To this day people believe the base still operates in the underground tunnels because of new power lines that were put up after its official closing. Researcher and human rights supporter John A. Quinn was able to confirm with Long Island Power Authority (LILCO) and its servicemen that there was an absurdly high usage of electric and energy coming from the base during 1996. That would be odd because according to the *Pioneer* (the official newspaper of Montauk), a small group of adventure seekers who chose to remain nameless for fear of trespassing penalties, visited the base at 1 a.m. on March 17, 1996, and although they found nothing sinister, did notice that the six large turbines that used to power the base had been torn down. So why the large use of electricity? The servicemen continue to state how odd it is that a New York State Park is using such high amounts of electricity with no visible reason to explain it. As late as 2017, Gil Carlson, the author of *Montauk Project*, claims that not only is all of this bizarre and true, but the base is still covertly alive and active!

Further, while much of the base is open to the public today, there are still areas that are off-limits because of "Unstable Dangerous Structures" and, as the park pamphlet explains, "Unexploded Ordinances" lying around. In other words, there are still some munitions that can detonate in this public park, even though park officials hired a private contractor to the tune of $550,000 to search for and remove them.

Was the Montauk Project just an urban legend created by overactive imaginations that became a catchall for every far-reaching sci-fi theory imaginable? Or is this the work of a government cover-up involving many branches, many scientific minds, and military intelligence, all trying to get their hands on the latest weapons of war?

The fact remains that we the people do not know everything that is going on. If someone had talked about the Manhattan Project while it was happening, people would have scuffed it off. Eventually however, once a technology becomes widely known, secrecy is discarded and projects and documents are declassified and made public.

To this day, two men, Preston Nichols and his coauthor and publisher, Peter Moon, have made it their mission to reveal as much as they can about the Montauk Project. They say that "Long Island is like a big Area 51. It's loaded with secrecy . . . and if you don't have an understanding of the human mind on a quantum level, then all of this sounds like hogwash." Hogwash or not, this duo has interviewed hundreds of people around the world, intelligent engineers and scientists, who claim they've witnessed things during their work on the Montauk Project. Why would these respected people put their reputations on the line and risk being thought of as nuts? Filmmaker Christopher Garetano in his film, *Montauk Unveiled,* has caught many of these "outrageous and fantastic" eye-witness "subjects" on film as well. What is the truth? As with many government conspiracy theories, we may never really know.

But either way, it is one heck of a story to tell while picnicking on the lawn in Camp Hero State Park way out on Montauk Point, just a stone's throw away from the lighthouse.

CHAPTER 4

Typhoid Mary: The Killer Cook

On August 1906, Charles Henry Warren, a wealthy New York banker, thought it would be wonderful to take his family on vacation to the upscale Oyster Bay area on Long Island. Since he was used to having an impeccably kept home and the servants to provide it, he brought along a staff, which included maids, a gardener, and a cook. In total there was an entourage of eleven people staying in the luxurious rented villa.

Early into the vacation Warren became unhappy with his cook and discharged her on August 4. He replaced her with Mary Mallon, another cook highly recommended by the employment agency.

Mary was a blonde, blue-eyed, buxom, thirty-seven-year-old Irish immigrant who loved her job. She had worked for wealthy families all over New York, often as the chief and most trusted member of the staff. Mary was at the top of the domestic service ladder, earning a nice living.

On August 27, three weeks after Mary's arrival, tragedy struck. Warren's youngest daughter came down with extremely contagious typhoid fever and nearly died. In short succession, Mrs. Warren, two maids, the gardener, and another of Warren's daughters also contracted the illness. Six of the eleven members of the household were now ill with the deadly disease. Mary left their employment without notice, afraid she too might become afflicted. She went to work for another wealthy Park Avenue family.

Back in Oyster Bay, the family underwent weeks of high fevers, headaches, coughs, delirium, and noxious diarrhea. Luckily, they all survived.

News of the typhoid fever outbreak in this prestigious neighborhood was not as quick to go away as Mary. There had never been a case of typhoid in Oyster Bay before. This beautiful home was a world away from New York City's Lower East Side, which was overflowing with poor immigrants and reported to be more crowded than Calcutta, just as dirty, and a hotbed of disease. Thousands were dying of typhoid, intestinal illnesses, tuberculosis, whooping cough, and diphtheria.

By this time, scientists had made huge advances in the study of bacteriology, which allowed them to reexamine the cause of some of these diseases. Louis Pasteur and Robert Koch shocked the scientific world by proving that microbes invisible to the naked eye caused disease. By the late 1800s, researchers had identified the organisms that caused such diseases as leprosy, malaria, tuberculosis, cholera, and typhoid. But the notion that specific germ entities caused certain diseases was new to the layman, the uneducated, and some die-hard scientists, who still believed that disease was caused by "sewer gases" and the "Miasma" (aka pollution).

The New York City Department of Health was determined to find the source of the Oyster Bay case to prevent it from spreading. They knew two things for certain: that typhoid fever was transmitted by the ingestion of food or water contaminated with the feces of an infected person, and that they were looking for the bacteria known as *salmonella typhi.*

Methodically, health officials investigated the Oyster Bay house. They checked to see if contaminated toilet water leaked into the household plumbing. They checked the incoming milk delivery supply. They checked the household manure pit, the outhouse, the trash, and the sewage. An old lady immigrant who had sold the family clams was examined, but this possible source of the disease also proved to be a dead end.

The Department of Health was stumped. Rumors spread that the house itself was contaminated. This was not welcome news to the Thompsons, the owners of the house, who knew that if they didn't solve the typhoid mystery, no one would want to rent their house and they wouldn't be able to pay the mortgage.

In 1907 they hired a thirty-seven-year-old, freelance civil sanitary engineer, Dr. George Soper, to find the cause of the outbreak. Soper, a narrow-faced man with a trimmed mustache and receding hairline, fancied himself a Sherlock Holmes of sorts, who could track down the source of any disease in a city. He wondered if the Health Department had thoroughly questioned everyone in the household and found that there had been one member overlooked. Soper's dogged interview tactics revealed new information: One of the servants remembered that Mary Mallon had been a cook in the household for three weeks before and during the outbreak.

Soper, acquainted with the latest news in bacteriology, remembered reading that the incubation period for typhoid fever was three weeks, the same amount of time it took for Mary to go to work for the Warrens, and the family to show symptoms of the fever. He also knew that the disease could be spread by human hands touching food, after having come in contact with the stool of an infected person, who harbored the bacteria in his or her intestinal tract. If the infected person, say a cook, did not scrub his or her hands well, especially under the nails and behind jewelry, then the bacteria could be transferred onto food. Soper felt he had found the cause of the outbreak in Oyster Bay, the proverbial "smoking gun."

Like a dog on a scent, he went to the employment agency and starting reading through Mary's references and gathering information. He learned that, "She was a pretty good cook, but not particularly clean in her work habits." He also discovered that from 1900 to 1907, Mary had worked at seven jobs. In the seven households where Mary had worked, twenty-two people had contracted typhoid fever, including one young girl who died a few weeks after Mary came to work. But two other things struck Soper as odd: First, there was a two-year gap in her employment records, so he questioned how she could survive with no income. Second, Mary was reportedly as healthy as a horse!

A healthy person did not fit the profile of known typhoid carriers. All the typhoid cases he was aware of involved sick people transferring the disease, usually in dirty homes. Then it hit him. He remembered reading about one of Dr. Robert Koch's cases in Germany, where a healthy bakery owner was believed to have spread the disease to her customers. Mary could be a healthy carrier, a person who had had the disease at one point, recovered, but still had the bacteria living in her body. This would destroy the theory that filth in and of itself was the cause of the disease. If Soper could prove this hypothesis, Mary Mallon would be the first person in the United States to be identified as a healthy typhoid fever carrier. The discovery would put him on the scientific map, since this theory had not yet been proven or accepted by the US medical community. He was determined to track her down, get a stool sample, prove his theory, solve the mystery of this lethal problem, and thus become a hero.

By March of 1907, Soper had tracked Mary to her new place of employment at Walter Bowen's Park Avenue home. He had gotten a tip that a young daughter had just died in that house and the nurse who had taken care of her had taken ill as well. Soper felt he had caught Mary red-handed.

Soper visited the residence, and a chambermaid led him to Mary in the kitchen. After a few pleasantries, Soper blurted out, "Mary, without your knowledge you may be the cause of the outbreak at the Oyster Bay residence . . . I just need a few urine, feces and blood specimens to confirm my suspicions." He explained his theory. Mary argued that she was healthy, had never been sick a day in her life, and challenged him to explain how it was that she had worked for other families that had not gotten typhoid. To prove that she wasn't the carrier, she told him that she had lived with a family in the Bronx, where she had shared a room with both the adults and the children, and that none of them had gotten typhoid. Mary, feeling that Soper was desperate to use an immigrant, any immigrant, as a scapegoat to solve the case, refused to cooperate. They were at a stalemate. By now thoroughly angered, Mary picked up a carving fork and threatened to stab Soper with it if he didn't leave the residence immediately. Soper, calling from a safe distance, vowed he'd be back.

Armed with all the information he felt he needed to prove Mary was the carrier, Soper went to New York City Health Commissioner Hermann Biggs. Biggs was a proponent of the new science of bacteriology and was as determined as Soper to get a sample from Mary at all costs. Biggs also had the authority to order people to be vaccinated against their will if he felt they were a threat to society and could put the infirm under house arrest if necessary. In drastic cases, he could force a person into quarantine on various New York Harbor islands if he considered that person a health risk to the general population. Biggs' one goal was to wipe out the massive disease in New York City.

Biggs assigned Josephine Baker, one of the New York City Department of Health's trained doctors who also doubled as a field inspector, to get the specimens from Mary. He reasoned that sending a woman would make Mary more willing to cooperate.

Baker showed up at the Park Avenue residence prepared for a fight. She was accompanied by five policemen and an ambulance slightly hidden from view. Baker informed Mary that she needed to provide a sample to the testing lab at Willard Park Hospital and that Baker was there to insist that she go. Mary refused, and determined not to be a guinea pig, ran and hid. After several hours, the furious Baker spotted her hidden behind a hallway door. The five policemen, Baker, and the ambulance crew grabbed Mary and dragged her, kicking and screaming, to the ambulance. Baker sat on top of the feisty Irishwoman all the way to the infectious disease hospital.

Mary was furious, saying, "I have committed no crime, and I am being treated as an outcast, a criminal. It is unjust, outrageous, uncivilized. I am being held against my will." Finally, however, she cooperated with the examiners. Just as Soper had suspected, the test results showed that Mary was infected with typhoid bacilli. Later at the hospital Soper explained to Mary that she must have contracted typhoid at some point during her life, but passed it off as a common cold. The problem remained, however; although the disease did not affect her, the bacteria still existed in her body, which made her a healthy carrier. It also made her as contagious as a carrier who was visibly sick.

Mary had fulfilled her end of the bargain and wanted to go home. Since there was no legal precedent for dealing with a healthy person who was infecting the population, the Health Department decided to keep her in the hospital until they could decide what to do with her. Then the media got hold of the story and Mary made front-page news. The public was on Mary's side because she was outwardly healthy, being kept against her will, and being prevented from earning a living.

Soper, too, was not sure of his next move. Eager to find out how Mary got typhoid, he tried to find an answer by visiting her rented room on Third Avenue near 33rd Street looking for clues. Briehof, the saloon owner who rented to Mary, and who turned out to be her boyfriend, wasn't talking. Desperate for information, Soper devised an unprecedented tactic: He went back to the hospital and offered to pay Mary all the profits from a book if he could write about her experiences. Since in those days people didn't sell their "life stories" to the media, Mary thought that was ridiculous and refused his offer.

Meanwhile, health officials had had to make a decision. The New York City Department of Health released this statement to the press: "Civil liberties have to sometimes be bent for the public good. And while it may be perceived as a conflict, most serious people in public health and, in the country, would understand that depriving an individual of her freedom for, hopefully, a brief period of time, that's a legitimate step to take."

Without a trial, without legal representation, without any kind of due process, they placed Mary on North Brother Island, which is in the East River a few hundred yards from the South Bronx. The island was the largest place of quarantine in the city and was filled with hundreds of patients with infectious diseases, who were destined to stay there until they were either cured or died. Perfectly healthy Mary was given a small cottage and a dog to live with

Abandoned buildings on North Brother Island located in the East River between the Bronx and Riker's Island. Typhoid Mary, the first healthy US citizen confirmed as a typhoid carrier, was confined here for over two decades.

away from the general population. She was cut off from everyone and everything she knew.

The press had a field day with this. While the Department of Health felt it was justified, some doctors were outraged. Dr. Milton Rosenau from Washington, D.C., who was the director of the National Hygienic Lab, and other scientists voiced their objections to Mary's forced incarceration. They suggested to the Department of Health that instead of imprisoning her, they should help her find another kind of job, and get her to agree to refrain from cooking, so that she "won't be a danger to anybody."

Instead, the Department of Health decided to force Mary to take experimental drugs like Urotropin for three months. They told her if she took it, it would kill the bacteria and she could be set free. Mary took it, but she felt that that drug was killing her and stopped. She did research and found out that the drug was used for kidney problems (and urinary tract infections), not typhoid.

They then told her that if she agreed to have her gallbladder removed, which was probably the cause of her infection, it would most likely cure her and she could go home. Mary refused to undergo the surgery, saying, "No knife will be put on me. I've nothing the matter with my gallbladder." (It turns out she was right, and that there was a good chance she would have died from the surgery.—Thank goodness she was feisty and willing to stand up to doctors at that time, something that was not usually done.)

But the stress of her situation took a toll on Mary, emotionally, spiritually, and physically. She began to twitch and her left eye was paralyzed for six months. She complained that the Department of Health didn't so much as give her an eye patch.

Like a caged bird, Mary wanted to regain her freedom. She started a letter-writing campaign, repeatedly asking Soper, Baker, and Biggs to let her go. She said, "Why should I be banished like a leper and compelled to live in solitary confinement? Years of this life and I will be insane." Mary was determined to get justice.

But Soper was just as determined to save the city from her, so he dug deeper into Mary's past. He found that she had changed her name a couple of times, which explained her supposed two-year lapse in employment, since she was working under a different name. He asked himself why she had done this. Was she afraid that she wouldn't get hired if she was known to have been employed in many households with typhoid? What was her explanation for the fact that this disease followed her everywhere?

For two years Mary was kept isolated on Brother Island. In June 1909, an Irish attorney, George O'Neill, stepped forward and filed a law suit with the New York Supreme Court on Mary's behalf, demanding her freedom on the basis that she was healthy, was imprisoned without having committed a crime, and had never received due process.

The case now became of interest to publishing guru William Randolph Hearst, who published Mary's story in his paper the *New York American* on June 20, 1909. It was in this paper's headline that she was dubbed "Typhoid Mary." Unfortunately, the name stuck. Cartoons appeared that depicted her seasoning her cooking with tiny skulls of death. Mary was now thought of as a killer cook.

Since sensational stories sell papers, Hearst kept reporting on her. In the process some other amazing facts were revealed. Mary was not the only healthy carrier in New York. William Park, head of the bacteriological lab that had done the testing on Mary at the request of the Department of Health, came forward and said that there were over fifty other healthy carriers in New York, and some were involved in the food industry as well. The attorney asked the court why Mary was the only one quarantined.

The public now believed Mary was being targeted because she was Irish and a woman. In Mary's words, "I have become a peep show for everybody. Even the interns [on the island] come to see me and ask about the facts already known to the whole wide world. The tuberculosis men would say, 'There she is, the kidnapped woman.'"

The court agreed to hear Mary's case. The Department of Health justified its actions by stating that she was a menace to public health as indicted by the string of sick families she left behind.

Mary, however, had a few tricks up her own sleeve. While she was confined to the island, she used her boyfriend, the saloon owner Briehof, as her personal messenger. She had him send her stool and urine specimens to the Ferguson Lab in Manhattan.

According to that lab, no traces of typhus bacilli were found in Mary's stool or urine, in direct contradiction to the Department of Health's lab reports. The Department countered that not all specimens of a healthy carrier would contain the bacteria. Judge Mitchell Erlanger of the New York State Court ruled against Mary, believing she was still a "danger to society."

Mary stayed incarcerated until 1910, when a new health commissioner, Ernst J. Lederle, became involved with the case. Luckily for Mary, he disapproved of the situation from all angles: political, medical, and humanitarian. On February 19, 1910, he made Mary a deal. He agreed to set her free with the provision she sign an affidavit that stated that she "[was] prepared to change her occupation (that of cook), and would give assurance by affidavit that she would upon her release take such hygienic precautions as would protect those with whom she came in contact, from infection."

Mary agreed. Upon signing, she was removed from quarantine and allowed to return to the mainland. To help her out even further, Lederle arranged a new job for Mary as a laundress, which, unfortunately, was the lowest of jobs for working-class women. Financially, this was a far cry from the living she was used to making as a cook.

Her boyfriend helped her out monetarily, but soon after her release he died. Now Mary was alone, and could not make ends meet. She knew the Health Department was watching her every move. She had to report to them with details of where she was working and in what capacity. She reported from 1910 to 1913, but then she got fed up.

In 1914 she didn't report and to her relief, the Health Department didn't notice. They had to monitor other cases; almost three percent of the population was now designated as healthy carriers. There was neither the money nor the manpower to keep track of everyone, so they chose to target only those healthy carriers in the food industry. Unfortunately for the Health Department, that number was in the thousands.

Mary was worried about her survival. She changed her name to Mrs. Brown, and against her sworn affidavit, went to work as a cook at the Sloane Maternity Hospital in March 1915. It didn't take long for her to appear again on Soper's radar. The hospital reported an outbreak of typhoid fever to the Health Department;

twenty-five people, including mothers, newborn babies, doctors, and nurses, had been infected and two had died.

Soper and Baker went to the hospital to investigate, and were surprised to find Mary posing as Mrs. Brown, but they would have to return with the proper paperwork before they could detain her for violating her affidavit. Caught red-handed, Mary didn't show up to work the next day. Soper and Baker traced Mary to her new home in Queens. When she didn't answer the doorbell, they put a ladder up to the second-floor window, fed meat to the barking dog, broke in, and told Mary she had to go with them. This time Mary went without a fight.

The newspapers detailed Mary's capture. They had lost all sympathy for her, calling her a "knowing perpetrator of pain, death and evil" or an "evil angel." Although some believed that she was just trying to survive, others felt she knowingly hurt people, making her equal to a murderer. Was Mary a victim or a villain? Other known "healthy" carriers were being exposed at that time, like food handler Tony Labella who infected 122 people with typhoid fever, five of whom died, yet Mary was the only one ever imprisoned. Justice should be blind and served the same to all.

Mary was sentenced to life on North Brother Island. Not wanting to live in isolation in her cottage, she took a job at Riverside Hospital as a lab technician. Over time, the Department of Health allowed her infrequent, monitored day trips to New York City to visit friends; Mary always returned to her prison home on time. In December 1932, she had a stroke that left her paralyzed and confined to a bed in the children's ward of the hospital, where she died on November 11, 1938, at the age of sixty-nine. An autopsy showed she was still a carrier at the time of her death.

During her entire life, Mary refused to believe that she had infected anyone with typhoid fever. In one of her final statements she said, "I lived a decent and upright life until I was seized, locked up and rechristened Typhoid Mary. Before God, and in the eyes of decent men, my name is Mary Mallon." Was this ignorance or denial? Either way, the fact remains that forty-seven people were infected and three people died at her hands.

Luckily, incidence of the disease has fallen sharply thanks to antibiotics and simple sanitation techniques like hand washing.

As for Riverside Hospital on North Brother Island, after Mary's death, it served as housing for WWII vets who were studying at city universities (beginning in 1946), and in the 1950s as a drug treatment center for adolescents addicted to heroin. Eventually it was abandoned and closed in 1963 due to corruption. In the 1970s the city tried to sell the island to the highest bidders, but the Board of Estimates, led by the then New York attorney general Bob Abrams, blocked the sale, stating it should remain a public parcel. Since 2001 the New York City Council's Parks Committee has controlled the island and designated it a sanctuary for the birds.

Not exactly sure how happy the birds are, but today this asbestos-filled, rubble-heaped, rat-infested, once-diseased island is patrolled and off-limits to the curious public who might want to take a peek at Mary's cottage. Signs warn of imprisonment and high monetary fines for those who dare to set foot on the once famous home of the diseased.

With modern technology, however, one can take a peek at the island, with its overgrown ivy vines swallowing the morgue and other buildings, through drone videos posted online, which supposedly have followed category A, no fly zone regulations, so that they don't interfere with incoming planes, lest they be fined.

In 2016, there was a short flurry of media talk of opening the "last unknown place in New York City" for tours to the public, but that has died down because of the expense necessary to get the island up to speed to safely accommodate hoards of adventure-seeking visitors. With nature reclaiming the island, a lot of TLC (like building new docks, getting rid of debris, fixing the hazards of falling bricks, and spending millions of dollars in restoration) would be needed before even the toughest of New Yorkers would want to trek through poison ivy and kudzu to get a glimpse of the past.

So for now, after fifty years of isolation, the island remains quarantined from its robust neighbors, with only the birds being able to hear the screams of laughter, blasts of concert music, and ice cream trucks only a stone's throw away from what once was the island of death.

CHAPTER 5

The Legends of Hell Gate

Adriaen Block loved a challenge and in 1614 he got just that as he sailed his forty-two-foot yacht the *Onrust* (Dutch for restless) across the treacherous waterway. Laughing at his ability to maneuver through it, he named the strait "Hellegat," which in Dutch can mean two things: "Bright Gate" or "Hell Gate."

Shortly after, other bold captains tried to run the gauntlet of Hell Gate and repeat Adriaen's feat, but not many were as lucky. One captain's log dating back to the early 1700s described the waterway, saying, "It is a key gateway to the Atlantic, marked with a giant whirlpool, punctuated with rocks, reefs and islands." After thousands of seamen lost their vessels to the perilous waters, the name Hell Gate stuck.

Few waters in New York hold as much turmoil, mystery, nautical disaster, and gold as Hell Gate, a narrow tidal strait located in the East River at the confluence of the Harlem River in New York City. From Manhattan, Hell Gate runs from 90th to 100th Streets. It connects Long Island Sound with New York Harbor and is surrounded by Manhattan; Queens; and three islands, Wards, Randall's, and Roosevelt. The waterway also separates Astoria, Queens, from Randall's Island and Wards Island, which are now one island connected by landfill. Known for its heavy currents, narrow berth, and humongous rocks, it has been the source of many legends through the centuries.

From the beginning, any captain worth his salt has known that this perilous one-mile passage is hellish due to the fact that the East River is actually a tidal stream whose tides conflict with the waters in Long Island Sound. As one engineer, Claude Rust, explained in 1971, "When the tide rises on the eastern seaboard it sets into New York Harbor and, farther to the northeast, into Long Island Sound. At New York Bay it splits at the tip of Manhattan, one current pushing up the Hudson and through the Harlem River, the other entering the East River. Here, with the horizontal movement impeded by the opposite flow of the Harlem River and the narrowness of the channel up to the Sound, the huge basin of Hell Gate begins to fill. The waters, like wild beasts, circle their confines, impatient for the chance to escape. The down coming flow of the Harlem River is then stopped by the strength of the escaping currents and sent back up through Little Hell Gate and the Bronx Kills, and the channels to the west, like a sluiceway, are filled with swift seething water racing up to the Bronx shore. This flow continues for hours, building up to a high tide along the East River shore. Then at a time when other waters would settle into slack, the down coming tide, which has been delayed four hours by the distance and the drag of the Long Island Basin, begins its relentless drive—and the struggle for mastery is on."

For centuries, there have been only two other choices for captains on this route: Take the long way around and avoid Hell Gate, or keep a ship idle, waiting for the tide to change, and waste time and money in the process. Since to impatient captains, neither of these choices was a good one, many ships suffered a horrible fate.

One of the most famous ships ever consumed by the treacherous appetite of Hell Gate waters was the HMS *Hussar*. The *Hussar* was a British frigate, a warship built for speed and maneuverability, that carried twenty-eight guns, as well as a full crew of officers, men, slaves, and prisoners. Its main mission was to instill fear, destroy enemy ships (which happened to be the American and French during the Revolutionary War), and take their treasures for the British forces. The *Hussar* was very successful at its job, and was loaded with gold, silver, and precious gems from other ships it had destroyed.

In the late fall of 1780, the *Hussar* was anchored in New York Harbor off of an area known as the Battery, when a series of unfortunate events influenced the fate of the ship. At that time, New York was still controlled by the British, so a number of American patriots imprisoned for rebellion were held captive on "prison ships" docked at Wallabout Bay along the northwest shore of the borough of Brooklyn. Sources vary as to why the captain of the *Hussar*, Charles Pole, was obliged to take on seventy of these prisoners, some of whom were officers in the American Army.

Captain Pole also became obliged to take on the entire cargo of another frigate, the HMS *Mercury*, a treasure ship that had just been commissioned into battle. The *Hussar* was now heavily overweight. Adding to the captain's problems, the French, who had just joined forces with General George Washington's troops north of the city and were not happy that the *Hussar* had sunk and pillaged some of their ships, were in hot pursuit.

Bulging at the seams, and in danger of being overtaken by the enemy, the unlucky *Hussar* was instructed to depart toward Long

Island Sound and dispatch rations and payroll to the British army. On Thursday, November 23, 1780, the man-of-war *Hussar* left the Battery and headed toward Gardiner's Bay on eastern Long Island with two hundred people and about $25 million on board.

With the French fleet in close pursuit, the captain sought the advice of a slave pilot named Swan as to the best route to take to Gardiner's Bay. The captain could have taken the longer, safer way around by exiting New York harbor into the Atlantic Ocean, but instead decided to take the short cut through Hell Gate, ignoring the expert advice of Swan, who had navigated those dangerous waters many times before. Swan bluntly told the captain the ship would not make it. But Captain Pole ignored him and forged ahead.

Slowly, the *Hussar* made her way up the East River, where it was bounced back and forth. It was about 3 p.m. when it happened: The currents smashed the bow of the ship into Pot Rock, a sharp protuberance that lay ten feet under the surface, just opposite the upper extremity of Randall's Island. At first there appeared to be no real damage, so they kept heading up the Sound instead of trying to land on Randall's Island. But then the situation changed. All of a sudden, the ship started to take on water. The captain tried to land the *Hussar* on Stony Point and Port Morris (or Manhattan Island as it was then called) but unfortunately, they were out of time. At 7 p.m. in "currents of 9 knots," and just a mere one hundred yards from shore, the vessel sank instantaneously. It was still intact.

Out of the two hundred people on board, only sixty crew members survived. The ship, its dead prisoners, and the estimated $25 million lay seventy-two feet below water in a rocky grave near 135th Street in the Bronx.

The haunted Hell Gate Bridge spans 1,017 feet and connects Wards Island and Astoria, Queens, New York, providing direct transit from New England to New York City. Once considered the most durable bridge in the world, it spans the perilous Hell Gate waters where the HMS *Hussar* sank with $1.5 billion in treasure.

Because there was a little thing called the Revolutionary War going on, the British government did not immediately recover its sunken treasure from the devil's lair. In fact, it denied that there was any treasure on board at all, some say as a cover-up to keep treasure seekers away. The ship lay there, untouched by the British government for fourteen years.

Finally in the spring of 1794, when things had settled down, the British government was able to turn its attention to the recovery. They dispatched two brigs from England, fully equipped with divers, a large diving bell, and other tools needed for underwater exploration. Once at Hell Gate, the British realized that the recovery would not be an easy task. The diving bell was ineffective because of where the ship lay, in an area where the current was running at full velocity. They reached the deck of the ship, but could not get near the hold, the lower part of the interior hull where important storage like gold was kept.

After two years of constant trial and error, the British abandoned the project, but offered a large salvage reward to anyone who could recover the treasure. In 1819, Major Baied of the US Navy formed a private company to retrieve the treasure. He, too, armed his expedition with men and a diving bell and attempted to pick up where the British government had left off. But after two years and $30,000, his company only managed to get a few cannons off the vessel. For the next twenty-five years, various companies tried and failed to get the treasure using the diving bell method.

In 1850, a man known as Captain Taylor devised a new plan for retrieving the treasure using a seventy-pound submarine armor suit with a glass-fronted copper helmet, tightly sealed rubber jacket and pants, and a hose that pumped fresh air to the diver. Taylor had invented this "diving suit" two years earlier and was using it successfully on other salvage expeditions in the Western Lakes, so he saw no reason why it shouldn't work with the *Hussar* treasure as well. He anchored his ship over the site of the wreck, and after just two months, had already gotten farther than other expeditions, managing to remove a portion of the *Hussar*'s deck that blocked access to the hold. But as timing would have it, the US Government took him off the job and put him to work on another ship that had sunk off of the Straits of Gibraltar. Taylor was anxious to get back to the *Hussar,* but unfortunately, he fell sick during the Gibraltar expedition and was unable to finish his attempt at the treasure.

Another enterprise, the Worcester *Hussar* Company, however, had been watching Taylor's progress. It knew Taylor was onto something and so in that same year, 1850, it decided to use his invention and invest six years trying to get the treasure. During that time, it managed to pull up an intact human skeleton, followed by several right arm bones with the chains and manacles still attached to the wrists, graphically revealing why none of the American prisoners or slaves had been able to escape.

Media interest also ran high. A *New York Times* reporter was allowed on board during one expedition, where he personally witnessed the retrieval of nineteen gold guineas in perfect condition, bearing dates from 1711 to 1776, as well as a solid lump of gold consisting of three guineas, a crown, and a half crown with silver in the center. The bulk of the estimated $25 million, however, was still tucked away securely in the hold, mainly because the ship had sunk near violent tides, and divers could only work at low tide, one to three hours a day, five months of the year.

Through the years, disputes over the legal ownership of the treasure were inevitable. During its expedition, the Worcester Company claimed that the British government had given up its entitlement to the recovery of the wreck and that the company owned the full amount of whatever it recovered. According to some sources, the British continued to claim that the treasure was theirs; it took nearly 200 years before the US government stepped in and ordered the British out, informing them that they no longer had rights to a ship in New York waters.

While treasure hunters debated who owned the underwater lottery ticket, ships were still meeting their watery graves at the entrance of Hell Gate and something had to be done about it. In 1851 the US Army Corps of Engineers began to clear obstacles out of the way, big obstacles, like the Pot Rock outcropping that downed the *Hussar,* to make the strait easier to navigate. This mammoth feat was accomplished with explosives, a difficult task that took over seventy years to complete.

At first the Army Corps tried above-ground explosives, but after a couple of attempts, they found that subterranean explosions would work better. The men dug tunnels branching downward from a cofferdam and under the river itself; these tunnels were packed with explosives and the reefs were detonated from below. Slowly but surely, they blasted away at nature's gate, and on October 10, 1885, the largest man-made explosion in human history went off, using 300,000 pounds of explosives that wiped out the flood rocks leaving nothing but memories. The megablast sent the water jetting 250 feet in the air and was heard all the way to Princeton, New Jersey. Although some cited other explosions, it was later said that the blast was "the largest planned explosion in destruction intensity until . . . the atom bomb was dropped over Hiroshima, Japan, in 1945!"

Either way it was a memorable ruckus at Hell Gate. What do you do with all that left-over rock? You fill in the water between two islands and create one big one. And that's what they did, making Mill Rock and Little Mill Rock one island joined forever, thus allowing ships a smoother passageway through Hell Gate.

With the new opening, some people now felt it would be easier to access the treasure. (Never mind the fact that the explosives might have blown it to smithereens.) Adventurers poured out of the woodwork. Some were so determined to find the legendary treasure that they invested all their money into its recovery. One such man was Simon Lake, the inventor of the modern submarine, who in 1935 put all of his assets into the search but found nothing.

In 1985 the *New York Times* reported that salvage expert Barry L. Clifford had used a sonar device similar to the one that helped find the *Titanic* to locate the underwater treasure, which was about 175 feet off the South Bronx shore, in "80 feet of murky water." At the time, Clifford said he was seeking state and federal permission to "remove debris and raise the wreck." But apparently that never happened. So the search continues to this day and why shouldn't it? If the treasure still exists, it's said to be worth between $800 million and $1.5 billion in today's market.

Many recent treasure seekers have had a passion for the history of the HMS *Hussar,* like author Robert Apuzzo, who spent a lifetime doing painstaking research on the ship. The person most actively looking for the treasure today is Joseph Governali, an actor with a big "Brooklyn type" personality whose stage name is Joey Treasures, and who appeared in *Die Hard 3*. He is also a real estate agent, treasure salvager, and the president of HMS *Hussar,* Inc.

In preparation for the hunt, Governali has studied rare books from the New York Public Library and Portsmouth Museum in Greenwich, England, uncovered diaries and memoirs, searched the archives on Gardiner's Island, and met with former Prime Minister Tony Blair and Robert Ballard, the man who found the wreck of the *Titanic*. He employs a maritime attorney, a dive team, and according to Governali "two of the finest archaeologists in the world, Duncan Mathison and James Sinclair," the second of whom is also the chief archaeologist on the wreck site of the *Titanic*, to analyze artifacts that his team has brought to the surface and identify them as belonging to the *Hussar.* On one dive, he retrieved an authentic Revolutionary War beer pitcher said to be the only one of its kind in the world. Governali keeps searching; he posted blogs on the Internet on July 23, 2010, and asked local antique and pawn shops in the New York area to notify him of artifacts that could be from the *Hussar.* In 2013 he shot a TV pilot called "Hells Gate Gold," in which the self-proclaimed "King of Hellgate" hired three dive teams and challenged them to compete to get to the treasure first, with the reward being a slice of the golden pie. In the pilot he recorded footage that he claims is part of the *Hussar* wreckage off the Tiffany Street Pier in the Bronx. He feels the wreckage has been pushed northward by storms. Governali feels he is getting closer to the treasure, and has had his attorney file "an arrest order on the ship in the Federal Admiralty Court." He claims to be "the first person . . . to have ever claimed a shipwreck in New York state waters." The theory that the treasure is still down there seems to be more fact than legend according to contemporary treasure seekers like Governali. Whether the bulk of the treasure still exists intact only time will tell. As late as 2017, Governali (under his pseudonym) has done follow-up videos for NATGEO on Vimeo called "Joey's Treasure and The Hell Gate Gang." Despite battling the currents, the lead diver on his first descent managed to somehow get a 1778 gold coin. As of this writing the search for the motherlode of gold continues.

But sunken ships aren't all that gives Hell Gate its devilish reputation. What about the ghosts? Legend has it that during low tide, a rock wall in the Hell Gate basin becomes visible when the water pulls back into the strait. The British soldiers were said to take their American prisoners into that area while the tide was low and chain them to the exposed rock wall. They would then board their ships and watch as the tidal flow silenced the screams of the drowning men. Years later, when the Hell Gate Lighthouse was built in 1829 on North Brother Island, the dangerous northern approach to Hell Gate (and later the home of the infamous Typhoid Mary), the keepers would tell tales of the ghostly shrieking of the murdered American rebels. After the waters had their way, little evidence would remain, only a skull or two washed ashore decades later. (Apparently this was a torture tactic during the Revolution, as in Long Island Sound there is an entire island called "Execution Rock" that was known for this very same punishment.)

And finally, to complete the legend, there's a haunted Hell Gate Bridge as well. In the early 1900s, a plan was conceived for a bridge that would make Hell Gate even more accessible and would also link the New Haven and Pennsylvania railways, creating direct passenger service from New York to Boston. Designer and overseer Gustav Linderthal finished building the longest, heaviest, strongest steel arch bridge in the world on September 30, 1916. Today the bridge is currently still on the list of longest steel arch bridges in the world, at number seventeen.

The Hell Gate Bridge became legendary like the waterway underneath. It is almost ten stories high, its main span crossing the East River at 1,017 feet, 6 inches, fabricated of 3.2 miles of steel.

The engineering was so precise on this bridge that when the last section of the main span was put into place for final adjustments it was only 5/16 of an inch off! Nazi demolition plans targeting the bridge were thwarted during World War II.

Originally the bridge carried four train tracks, two for passenger trains and two freight train tracks; one freight track was abandoned in the mid-1970s and that is where the ghostly legends above Hell Gate begin.

There are many tales of children and adolescents visiting the abandoned track and seeing the lights of a phantom train coming toward them. Most would run before the train ever got to them, but the more curious and brave who watched and waited for the phantom train to arrive reported seeing hundreds of the lost souls of Dutch and Spanish explorers disembark. Many other late-night adventurers claimed to have been chased down the tracks by the souls of the prisoners, slaves, and seamen who had been victims of the turbulent waters of Hell Gate below.

There were also more troubling stories of a homeless child molester who would kidnap children, blindfold them, and force them into the huge chamber located at the foot of the bridge. As the story goes, when the police finally figured out the location of the hell hole, they stormed the place armed and ready to drag the rapist to justice. When they got there, he was gone, but he had left behind traces of his brutal work; supposedly, areas of the chamber had wall-to-wall photos of the children being raped, and the stench is said to have sickened the policemen. Entering this chamber became a rite of passage for many New York teens.

Despite its grisly reputation, they tried to spruce up the bridge in the late 1990s with a "Hell Gate Red" paint job, the first repainting since the bridge opened in 1916. But whether the lost souls did not want happiness around this structure or it was just a flaw in the paint, when they switched it from lead-based to a new quick drying formula, the brightness quickly dissolved, leaving the bridge with its current day, "faded, splotchy appearance." At one point in 2013, the nonprofit New York Anti-Crime Agency was pushing to brighten it up again by adding lights to the non-functioning towers, but the Amtrak owners shot down the idea, saying the red lights above and below the bridge were enough, and any more light would become a "safety hazard for their engineers." So Hell Gate was once again destined to retain an unremarkable facade.

Despite its lackluster appearance, the well-built bridge was the inspiration for the Harbor Bridge in Sydney, Australia, the Tyne Bridge in England, and New York's Bayonne Bridge, which connects Staten Island and New Jersey. According to the February 2005 issue of *Discover* magazine, the Hell Gate Bridge "would be the last New York City bridge to collapse if humans disappeared, taking at least a millennium to do so [while] most other bridges would fall in about 300 years."

Today, Hell Gate still has a reputation, whether from its treacherous waters or from its haunted bridge. Some scoff and say that its navigational difficulty is more myth than fact, and while Hell Gate is considered difficult to navigate due to strong tidal flows, at certain points in the tidal cycle, the water goes slack, making it as calm as a lake—a good kayaker could pass through without much trouble. They claim that the danger is not in the rough waters but in the heavy water traffic around the area.

But attitudes like this can inspire false confidence in sailors. For example, there is a well-circulated local story that claims the current in the Gate makes it nearly impossible to hit the wall at 96th Street off of Gracie Mansion when westbound. Many an unattended vessel has broken away from its moorings and somehow been divinely guided through the waterways unscathed. But according to a third-generation tug master known as Captain Brucato, you can hit the wall, and if you misjudge your turn, depending on draft, wind, and speed, you will not only hit that wall with your vessel, but bounce across the river and hit Roosevelt Island's north end as well, as the current from Mill Rock throws your vessel across the river. This happened to a large tug towing a 130,000-ton barge; it careened into an oil barge, and then the two banged along the Upper East Side promenade until both were pinned to the wall at the 63rd Street Heliport.

For centuries, Hell Gate has been known to devour many a ship and thousands of lives. With its sunken treasures, perilous seas, vengeful ghosts, and phantom trains, it's still a mighty force to be reckoned with. Today the waterway continues to have a strong tidal flow, and even though at times the tidal cycle water goes slack, making it calm like a lake, don't be fooled—Hell Gate is still hell at times to get through. So sailors beware!

CHAPTER 6

The Mysterious Leather Man

Like clockwork, every thirty-four days, for thirty-one years, the children and housewives of forty-one towns from the Hudson to the Connecticut River would hear that familiar sound of squeaking leather. Slowly, a mysterious figure would appear out of the woods or mountains and walk silently toward their homes, the leather saying it all. Children who had never seen him would run in fear. But those who knew him would announce his presence, calling, "He's here!" With a welcome fit for a celebrity, food would be set out. The housewives he visited took pride in being one of hundreds to care for him. On the porch steps he would eat the hot meal in silence, nod, grunt, make a gesture of thanks, and be on his way. Children would put old faded pennies on the fence post for him in anticipation of his next visit and in return he would replace them with shiny new ones. Some villagers were able to capture his picture on film, but those who did so without his permission were never honored with his presence again.

Who exactly was this mystery man? He was known simply as "the Leather Man," aptly named, for all he wore 365 days of the year was an entire outfit—hat, clothes, shoes, and satchel—made from roughly sewn leather boot pieces. . He was five-feet-seven-inches tall and weighed 160 pounds, although he looked much bigger because the leather suit weighed sixty pounds. He never changed clothes, and was said to even bathe in that outfit. Tales of this punctual vagabond have circulated around the world. While many of the stories about him are folklore, he was a real homeless man who captured the imagination and sympathies of almost all who met him.

Every town that the Leather Man visited had stories about him. It's estimated there were over a thousand circulating about his true identity. The version that has been handed down from generation to generation is that the Leather Man's real name was Jules Bourglay and that he came from Lyons, France.

The story goes that in the early nineteenth century, Jules met and fell in love with a leather merchant's daughter named Margaret Laron. Jules, who came from a lower-class family than Margaret's, was set to be a wood carver. Because of the difference in their social class, Margaret's father objected to the match. But Jules was very much in love and convinced the father to take him into the company and teach him the leather trade. The father agreed under these conditions: If Jules proved to be a worthy businessman, he could have Margaret's hand in marriage; if he wasn't, the marriage would not happen.

At first Jules advanced in the firm. At one point, he became the sole purchaser of leather for the company, which was a position of great responsibility. Everyone was pleased and the marriage day was set. But in 1855, the price of leather dropped forty cents over night. Jules decided to purchase a ton of Persian leather at the low price; this decision resulted in the leather firm becoming bankrupt. Humiliated because he had brought this on himself, his bride-to-be, and the family that he loved, he became a lost soul wandering the streets of France, dressed in leather. Because of this mental breakdown, he was placed in a Paris monastery, from which he escaped two years later, subsequently vanishing from France never to be seen again.

Around this time, reports had come in about a man seen walking the streets of Harwinton, Connecticut, wearing an outfit made of leather patches. He would disappear, reappearing every thirty-four days in the same towns. When approached and asked by curious residents who he was, he would grunt and use hand gestures for most of his communication, for he spoke little English. He was a gentle soul, but it was obvious he wanted to keep his identity a secret, for if anyone asked him about his background, the conversation would abruptly end. The problem was, as with all secrets, the more mysterious you are, the more people want to know. So they began keeping track of this strange man's habits, hoping to gain insight into his odd behavior. Sightings of his arrivals would appear in the local papers.

From 1858, before Lincoln became president, until 1889, he established a pattern, a rigid, self-imposed walking circuit that consisted of 365 miles. He would never retrace his steps and would only travel in a clockwise direction. His circular route took him through many New York towns, including Yorktown, Peekskill, Somers, Brewster, and North Salem. He then went west into Connecticut to Ridgefield, Danbury, Bridgewater, Waterbury, Forestville, New Britain, Old Saybrook, Guilford, Branford, New Haven, Stratford, Bridgeport, Norwalk, New Canaan, Stamford, and Greenwich. Back in New York again, he traveled toward the Hudson through White Plains, Armonk, Chappaqua, Ossining, Mt. Kisco, Bedford

Hills, and Pound Ridge, where he would start the loop all over again. It took him exactly thirty-four days to complete the cycle. Some people assumed he walked nonstop, but it was learned that he only traveled ten miles a day, stopping for plenty of rest, drink, and food. People knew when to expect him down to the minute. It was often said that "housewives set their clocks by him."

How was it that someone without a home, a job, or a family could be so efficient and self-disciplined? Some say he was doing penance for what he believed was his unforgivable failure. No one will ever know. But he was a fascinating enigma to the people, who were more concerned about his food, health, and comfort than that of other unfortunates passing through the towns he visited.

This was an accomplishment, especially since, during this time, homeless people and tramps were considered such a widespread problem that a strict "tramp law" was established in 1879, promising indigents state imprisonment for a year. Public opinion was so set against these unwelcome visitors, according to historian Peter Hall, that some editors of the time declared the solution to the tramp problem was to poison their food or to take them out and shoot them.

It was essential, then, for the Leather Man to distinguish himself from the average tramp. Whether he did this consciously or not, we do not know. The fact is that he was a consistently punctual wanderer and this made him stand out from the rest. In addition, he knew how to take care of himself and get what he wanted. He patched his own clothes, made all of his utensils, and asked for nothing but a meal, some tobacco, and matches from the hundreds of residents he charmed along the way. This made him a local celebrity tramp of sorts, and in the towns on his route, exempt from the tramp law.

Not bad for a man who spoke little, mainly in grunts. But the Leather Man was a smart guest. He never overstayed his welcome. On his route he would choose a home, knock at the door, and motion his hand to his mouth for food. How or why he chose a certain home no one knows. But people didn't mind him because he was clean and obviously religious. Many assumed he was a Roman Catholic because he wore a religious medal, refused meat on Fridays, and had a French prayer book dated 1844. He also was not a nuisance. He would only ask for one meal from each house over thirty-four days. And while on occasion he might have his meals indoors, he never accepted an offer to spend the night at someone's home, no matter how bad the weather.

Instead, he knew nature like the back of his hand and would sleep at night in caves along his route. Curious children, who would secretly follow him, were the first to discover his cave-dwelling habits. The Leather Man was popular with children, who would often sit on a log next to him in silence as he ate.

It was noted that he was very clever in his living arrangements, especially when it came to heat. Before he would leave each cave to continue his walkabout, he would leave a tepee-like setup of small dry sticks, which would be placed on a large flat stone in the center of the cave. In essence, this was his hearth, and all he needed to do upon his next arrival was to light the sticks with matches. Within minutes of his arrival at any one of his dwellings, he'd be toasty warm.

He had a backup supply of dry wood that he stored in the crevices of rocks in the cave. He also had a supply of coal. He would warm it by the fire, and then when it was hot enough, he would sweep it outside the hearth and would use the deposit to improvise a soft, heavy, compact bedding having a cushiony "soapstone" feel to it. The final result with the cave overhang was like sleeping in a warm oven.

He did his own cooking at times, carrying all his worldly possessions and handmade tools in his satchel, including an axe, scissors, cooking pan, and eating utensils. Some of his nightly cave dwellings even had little gardens where he grew a few vegetables, while others had spaces for meat storage and fruit that he picked up along his treks. Whenever part of his leather attire wore out, he would pick up a piece at one of the many tanneries along the way and patch up his clothing. If his walking boots, which were made out of thick wooden soles nailed to leather uppers, wore out, he would make new ones from discarded boot tops. Some say he wore the outfit to be reminded of his life back in France; others say he was just being practical, using the leather to protect him from rain and harsh winters. Who knows why he didn't take the suit off in the summer.

He did buy things in various towns on occasion. Where he got or earned the money, no one knows. There were rumors that the Leather Man had a fortune buried in some of the caves, and that he was just an eccentric old man compelled, for some reason, to perform this 365-mile ritual. Could he have suffered from Obsessive-Compulsive Disorder (OCD)? One storekeeper at Harding's grocery store in Branford, Connecticut, kept an inventory of what he bought: "one loaf of bread, a can of sardines, one-pound of fancy crackers, a pie, two quarts of coffee, one gill of brandy and a bottle of beer." The same day, the Leather Man went down the road to the Chinsey residence and ate the meal they laid out for him. He obviously had a good appetite.

The Leather Man became so well known that he was commemorated in portraits, magazines, news accounts, and books. His name appeared in newspapers ranging from the reputable *New York Times* to the sensational *New York Herald.* In 1885 his walking schedule was published. While he was alive, merchants used his photo to advertise their goods. Families who were on his thirty-four-day rotation would save things he touched or sneak a picture and consider it a family heirloom. His name was more known than those of many hardworking farmers and businessmen, and yet he never spoke more than a dozen words.

Whenever the Leatherman was coming to town, the children in Westchester County, Putnam County, and Western Connecticut would recite the first paragraph of a popular seventeenth century English folklore rhyme about a farmer looking for his wife:

One misty moisty morning, when cloudy was the weather,
I chanced to meet an old man dressed all in leather.
I began to curtsey, he began to grin
And howdy do, and howdy do, and howdy do again.

Not everyone accepted his peaceful, though odd, existence so readily. There were stories of the men in some towns being suspicious of his motives. He was teased and harassed in a New Haven,

Connecticut, tavern, where some men hoped that by forcing liquor down his throat, they would get him drunk enough to divulge more about who he was. In Forestville, they tried to get him drunk as well, and when they couldn't, they threw him in a horse trough. From then on he avoided town centers and made sure to only travel country lanes and railroad routes to get to his destinations.

In 1887 it was reported that a raw sore had appeared on the Leather Man's lips. By 1888 people began to notice that the skin on his hands, face, and chest suffered from frostbite and was hard, swollen, and oozing blood. The government became concerned, and in 1888, thirty years after his first circular route, the Connecticut Humane Society arrested him and forced him to undergo psychological and medical examinations. He was taken to Hartford Hospital, where he was pronounced "sane except for an emotional affliction." Since he had money, desired his freedom, and knew how to take care of himself, they figured he was more odd than mentally ill. The sore on his lip was found to be cancer of the mouth from his tobacco habit. They tried to force him to stay and get medical attention, but within a few hours, he sneaked out of the hospital and was on his regular route once again.

After his arrest and examination, more articles appeared about him. Some papers looking for sensational headlines repeated the Jules Bourglay story. Others said he was an escaped convict who had murdered his wife and her lover. Those who knew him, however, were not frightened.

The year 1888 was not a good one for the Leather Man. Although he had done his route faithfully, summer, winter, spring, and fall, never missing a day in over thirty years, that year, during the Great Blizzard in which hundreds lost their lives, he slowed down to the point where he was four days off his regular schedule. Some say it was the weather, others say he stopped to make new shoes for himself because his old ones were worn out. Notices in the newspapers appeared with people being concerned he had perished. But when he appeared four days later everyone was relieved.

The next year his regular caretakers noticed his health declining. During his thirty-one years of travel, he had never seemed to age, but now he looked different. The lower left side of his lip was eaten away. When eating, he had to crumble his food into coffee, and he would constantly wipe his mouth with a patch of leather. It was during this year that he declined his favorite tobacco from all who offered it. Although in the past he had always seemed shy and a bit skittish, he was now visibly more nervous.

On March 24, 1889, Henry Miller brought his fiancée to George Dell's farm, to the Saw Mill Woods Cave in Mount Pleasant (Briarcliff) New York, near Ossining, to show her where the Leather Man stayed when he was in the area. To his shock, he found the body of the Leather Man crumpled in the cave. He was dead.

Miller notified the authorities. The Westchester County coroner determined the cause of death to be cancer of the mouth due to chewing tobacco. The Leather Man was believed to be sixty-five years old at the time of death. Because he had no known family, he was left in the public's charge for burial. The Globe Museum in New York City purchased his leather clothes.

The Leather Man, naked for the first time in thirty-one years, was put in a burial gown and placed in a plain pine box in the corner of Potters Field in Sparta Cemetery, on Route 9, off of

Scarborough Road in Ossining, New York, just 200 yards northeast of the Scarborough Presbyterian Church. His grave was marked by a simple iron pipe. His death made the front page of the obituary sections of the *New York Sun* and *Hartford Times.*

After his death, the Globe Museum tried to cash in on the Leather Man's notoriety. They hired a man to wear the leather outfit and frighten audiences by portraying him as mean and vicious. He would yell, "I am hungry, give me a child to eat!" Those who knew of the real Leather Man's gentle nature protested, and the performance was shut down. Shortly after, the suit either disappeared or was destroyed by a fire in the museum.

Although he was dead, his legend lived on. In the 1930s, he was featured in a *Ripley's Believe It or Not!* cartoon.

In 1953, the town of Ossining decided he should have a tombstone. A small, used tombstone with the following inscription replaced the iron pipe:

FINAL RESTING PLACE OF JULES BOURGLAY

OF LYONS, FRANCE

"THE LEATHER MAN"

WHO REGULARLY WALKED A 365-MILE ROUTE

THROUGH WESTCHESTER AND CONNECTICUT FROM

THE CONNECTICUT RIVER TO THE HUDSON

LIVING IN CAVES IN THE YEARS

1858–1889

The fascination with the Leather Man was and is so great, that the Ossining Historical Society put a marker on his grave and a New York State Highway Historical Marker on Route 9 to direct the curious to the cemetery, which is often scheduled as a school trip for local students.

Although his tombstone bears the name of Jules Bourglay, his true identity remains unknown. The claim that the Leather Man was Jules Bourglay first appeared in a story published in the *Waterbury American* on August 16, 1884; it was later proven false and retracted on March 25, 26, and 27 in 1889. Unfortunately, many did not see the retraction and the story lived on. Leather Man researcher Dan W. DeLuca uncovered the retraction in 2006 and has been trying to set the story straight since, but legends die hard. Other Leather Man researchers, including Chauncey Hotchkiss, Allison Albee, and Leroy W. Foote, have unsuccessfully spent time, effort, and money trying to identify the Leather Man. Since he was fluent in French, researchers speculate he was either from France, Jules LeClerc from Aix-en-Provence, according to some, or more likely from Canada.

A map showing the towns he visited and some of the two dozen caves he is said to have lived in is available on the Internet at www.dreadcentral.com/img/coldspots/092-04.jpg. There are three such caves in the New York area, one located at Ward Pound Ridge Reservation in Westchester County. If you walk into the park and follow Honey Hollow Road path past a thicket of trees, glacial rock, and the remnants of old stone walls, you will come to a 660-foot cliff called "The Overlook." A curator from the Trailside Museum will be happy to help you with directions, and there are one or two markers on the road. Another of his cave dwellings is said to be in Katonah at the intersection of Cherry Street and Bedford Road, and the third is Pop's Cave near the supposedly haunted Buckout Road in Westchester County.

Some people (including this author) have visited the caves to see if they can re-create his trail, but even wearing modern hiking boots, they claim it is a treacherous trek and find the folklore about this legendary man even more amazing. Others are more interested in getting a feel for what his life must have been like in the rock homes. Many accounts have claimed that the caves are haunted, especially his main cave in Black Rock State Park in Connecticut, along the Mattatuck Trail, and Pop's Cave near Buckout Road that also used to store ammunition during the Revolutionary War. Those who have dared to stay the night claim to have seen his ghostly figure settle peacefully next to them as they prepared to sleep in the cave. None have felt threatened.

But those who come with malicious intent, such as one curious treasure seeker who believed the stories of the Leather Man's fortune, have not received such a benign welcome. The treasure hunter chose to stay the night in the Leather Man's Watertown cave, hoping to locate the loot. He reported "a strange cold breeze" that snuffed out his torch, and that he clearly saw the Leather Man's ghostly figure appear, stand up, and gesture for him to leave. He did leave hurriedly and empty-handed.

Reborn every once in a while in the media, the legend lives on. A documentary on the Leather Man called *The Road Between Heaven and Hell* aired on Connecticut Public Television in 1984 and can be found on YouTube. Pearl Jam recorded a song called "Leatherman" on the B-side of their single *Given to Fly*, and *The Guinness Book of World Records* fastest talking woman, the author of this book, Fran Capo, penned a poem in 2018 in his honor that can be found on her website www.francapo.com and below.

But the story doesn't end there. On May 26, 2011, per a Westchester County court order, the Leather Man's 122-year-old grave was dug up and the coffin opened. The reason? A team of volunteer Connecticut archeologists, led by Nicholas Bellantoni, and in agreement with the Ossining Historical Society Museum (the group that owns the Sparta Cemetery where many revolutionary soldiers are buried) wanted to do forensic testing (mainly on site with portable equipment) on his bones to gather DNA and solve the mystery of who the Leather Man really was. But to their surprise, there were no physical remains left, not even a wisdom tooth, which ironically is one of the best places to extract DNA! After a three-day intensive search, only some coffin nails and soil from the decomposed casket remained. How fitting for a man who his whole life wanted his past to remain a secret!

Bellantoni reasoned that the "grading of the nearby route 9 in the early twentieth century may have affected his burial site. The Leather Man was interred in a shallow grave covered by asphalt, mere steps from the busy road. The coffin nails were found less than one foot below ground." The unsuccessful dig made national headlines.

Three days after the search on a hot Wednesday morning with more than forty people in attendance, the Leather Man was given a proper reburial. This time it was on a prominent, hilly, dignified section of Sparta Cemetery, where the nails that had been found in his original grave were buried in a pine coffin. A

The Leather Man's final resting place is in Sparta Cemetery off Route 9 in Scarborough, thirty miles north of New York City. The original tombstone was just five feet off the main road on the left as you entered in the pauper section. But on May 26, 2011, the court allowed the body to be exhumed to test for DNA. No human remains were found in the coffin, so just the nails that were found were reburied in a pine casket under this boulder, which serves as his headstone.

large boulder from a construction site in Croton serves as his headstone and bears a bronze plaque with just two words, "The Leatherman." Near the massive stone stands a sign that reads, "Legends and Lore—The Leatherman. For no known reason from 1883 to 1889 he trod a 365-mile loop every 34 days between NY and CT clad in 60 pounds of leather. New York Folklore Society, William Pomeroy foundation 2016."

Reverend Timothy Ives of Scarborough Presbyterian Church conducted a short funeral service. Leather Man biographer Dan

DeLuca placed four pennies on the pine coffin before it was placed in the ground in tribute to the ritual the children used to do when the Leather Man came to town. Deluca's twenty-two years' of research led him to write a very detailed book, The Old Leatherman, complete with the Leather Man's routes mapped out, pictures of the houses he visited, and clippings from newspapers chronicling his whereabouts.

Despite their disappointment over the research team's inability to locate and identify the Leather Man's remains, many felt the reburial provided some closure and allowed them to pay proper respects to the larger-than-life man. Others, like Donald Johnson, a history teacher from Bethany, Connecticut, felt this solitary individual should have been left alone to rest in peace, which prompted him to create a website called, "LeavetheLeathermanAlone.com. Tons of newspaper articles in towns all along the Leather Man's trails carried articles in 2011 spouting various opinions about exhuming his remains.

After the reburial in May of 2011, the team went back once again in July 26, 2011, to the original gravesite to try to find any missed remnant of his physical being. All that was found was a golf ball.

In the annals of folklore, the Leather Man is right up there with Johnny Appleseed. Both were real wanderers whose life stories have become a tangle of fact and fiction, and so the mystery continues. Long live the Leather Man, a person who proved you don't have to have money to be famous and carefree.

"Ode to the Leatherman" by Fran Capo © 2018
(1839–1889)

The Leatherman, The Leatherman a legend would be told
about a silent stranger who would walk to parts unknown.
He'd trek from Hudson to Connecticut, and places in
    between
and grab a bite of food to eat that would give his body steam.

Punctual was his mark of fame, like clockwork on a wall,
the tick-tock counting thirty-four days, for thirty-one years
    in all.
Only wearing leather from his head down to his toes
he'd sleep at night in caves, along the routes he chose.

He spoke no word of English, but a Bible he did keep.
He meant no harm to anyone, and would grunt and leave
    to sleep.

Gentle was his nature, as all the households say.
This silent man was famous without the PR of today.
But just his odd behavior and reason for his trek,
would make the papers interested and so a log was kept.

Homeless he may be, and from France they say he came,
but never a true fact was known, not even his real name.

And when the Leatherman one day did not arrive,
a gentleman and lady found him dead inside his hive.

And so the man was buried without the clothes he wore,
a spectacle was made of him, which many fans abhorred.

And when the public cried about the shallow place he laid
the court exhumed his body, but found nothing in his grave.
So now some nails are buried on a hill beneath a rock;
the mystery continues with a plaque that marks his spot.

CHAPTER 7

The Lake Champlain Monster

Sandra Mansi grew up near Lake Champlain, a 125-mile freshwater lake shared by New York and Vermont, which also extends a few miles into Quebec, Canada. As a child, she and her siblings would go out in a boat on the lake with their grandfather to go fishing. To make sure the children behaved, he would tell them about the incredible serpent-like beast named Champ that lived in the lake and would eat bad children. He described a green, thirty-foot-long, slimy, scaleless beast with a long neck, snake-like body, and long pointy tail that would swish vertically to propel the creature. The children would eye the still waters around them and laugh nervously, not sure what to believe.

As an adult, Sandra moved to Connecticut, but she had fond memories of the lake near which she had grown up. On July 5, 1977, she, her two children, and her fiancé, Anthony, went on vacation near the lake. They parked the car along Lake Champlain's edge in New York, near the Canadian border, and walked down the rocky hill to the water. Sandra sat down on some rocks and the children went to play with buckets on the beach. Her fiancé went back to the car, only a few yards away, to get the camera to capture their pleasant outing.

As Tony got the camera, Sandra looked out onto the peaceful lake. Suddenly she saw motion at the surface. As she said later, "The lake started churning." At first she thought it was scuba divers, but there were too many bubbles located in one area. She thought it might be a school of fish, but soon dismissed that idea. As the area darkened near the surface, she saw a series of bumps. She thought that it might be a lake sturgeon, the largest freshwater fish in North America, which can weigh over 1,500 pounds, grow to lengths of over twenty feet, and live more than a hundred years.

While she pondered what this huge creature might be, it popped its head and neck out of the water about eight feet above the surface. It had a small head, a long neck, and a hump back. It moved its head from right to left, then turned and looked straight at her.

Instead of being frightened, she was in awe—there was Champ! Watching this magnificent-looking, prehistoric creature, she felt she had traveled back in time 65 million years. At that moment, she knew her grandfather hadn't been lying after all.

Her fiancé, however, didn't like the looks of the creature. He ran down to the beach, snatched the children up, and then grabbed Sandra's arm and pulled her from the rocks, insisting that she get in the car. Instead, Sandra snatched the Kodak Instamatic camera from his hands and took one quick photo of the beast. Her fiancé pulled her into the car and sped away. The whole sighting lasted about six or seven minutes. Sandra was happy; she had captured the beast on film for the world to see.

Sandra blew the photo up to an eight-by-ten, but worried people might think it was doctored. For a while, she kept it in a family album; a friend, however, convinced Sandra to ask an expert what the creature was. In 1980, she contacted Joseph W. Zarzynski, a former social studies teacher turned underwater archeologist and author, who had studied Champ and written several books about him based on over sixteen years of research. Zarzynski was impressed by the snapshot (the negative had been lost over time) and sent it to George Zug of the Department of Vertebrate Zoology at the Smithsonian Institution.

Zug determined that the creature didn't resemble any known animal in the lake or anywhere else in the world. The photo was sent to other experts at the University of Arizona to be analyzed for authenticity. A cryptozoologist, one who searches for animals considered legendary or otherwise nonexistent by mainstream biology, named Richard Greenwell, and other researchers digitized the picture and ran computer enhancement techniques on it to see if there

A photoshopped picture of Champ swimming in Lake Champlain. This photo hangs in the lobby of The Inn on the Library Lawn for the amusement of all its guests.
PHOTO COURTESY OF GARY GORMAN

was any evidence of hoaxing. They saw no pulleys or ropes and no superimposition. They concluded that whatever was in the picture had been in the lake at that distance, at that time. The late Richard Greenwell said that the unknown "object" in the water resembled a plesiosaur, a type of carnivorous aquatic (mostly marine) reptile. The plesiosaur had the same long neck, face, and body type as the creature in Mansi's photo.

Cryptozoologist Roy Mackal visited the lake in 1981 and thought that the creature might be a zeuglodon, a primitive form of whale with a long snakelike body. This matched the description of many other sightings, but not the Mansi photo. Whatever the creature was, it perplexed the researchers.

If either of these creatures existed, they reasoned, it would mean that somehow it had escaped extinction. What was in the lake was either a single animal at least ten thousand years old (a long time for something to survive) or there was a breeding population in the lake. A breeding population requires fifty adult creatures for short-term population survival and over five hundred to keep the population healthy for a long period of time. Could fifty large Champ-like creatures be living in the lake?

Mansi didn't care if there were one or five hundred creatures; all she knew was that something huge was living in Lake Champlain and she had the only photo in the world to prove it. The *New York Times* and *Life* magazine ran stories on her photo. To date, it is still the best shot of "Champ" that exists.

Over three hundred eyewitness accounts through the centuries have been chronicled. One YouTube documentary labeled "Lake Champlain Monster: Early 90s TV Segment" that was ripped off a decaying VHS tape of that show, chronicles eyewitness accounts with both photos and video evidence they had taken of Champ or at least what they believed to be Champ. These were all credible witnesses, from therapists to teachers to corrections officers. None were in search of Champ at the time, but were merely out for a day on the water at various locations. Each of these witnesses spotted an unknown beast and had the wherewithal to take photo or video footage.

According to this documentary, sighting #235 occurred on July 5, 1988, at Shelburne Falls by the husband and wife team of Walter and Sandra Tappen, a teacher and therapist, respectively, who took out their camcorder and started recording after the beast popped its head out, looked directly at them, and then dove back into the water. Within seconds it surfaced again nearer their boat. Sandra started screaming and jumped onto of the canopy of her boat. (Although I'm not quite sure how this is a survival maneuver.)

Sighting #301 occurred on July 9, 1992, at Bulwagga Bay, New York, by Frank Soriano, a corrections officer, who was with his wife on the way to a picnic and decided to stop and take a photo of the beautiful scenery. As he was snapping photos he saw "a snake-like body about twenty to thirty feet rise out of the water." He grabbed a video camera and started taping.

Sighting #211 occurred on June 30, 1985, at Badin Harbor by eyewitness Dennis Hall, an engineer who was out kayaking with his daughter. He shot video of Champ and described it as a "creature with a long neck and body the size of a Volkswagen." This encounter so convinced Dennis that Champ was the real deal that he formed Champ Quest with a friend, Richard Deuel. Champ Quest's sole purpose is to collect definitive evidence to prove the existence of Champ to the scientific community. They are convinced Champ is real. They look for feeding areas, and dive down to explore where the recorded sightings have occurred. They feel there is not one creature but a colony of them because the eyewitness reports have been going on for too long in history and too consistently for there to be one creature that has lived that long. (Now unless everyone is drinking the same Kool-Aid, all these eyewitnesses can't be hallucinating.)

Some say Champ is Lake Champlain's version of the Scottish Highlands Loch Ness Monster, Nessie. The first modern-day sighting of Champ (1873) predates the first modern-day reported sightings of Nessie (July 22, 1933) by sixty years.

The two legendary creatures share many of the same physical attributes and the lakes in which they live are similar as breeding grounds as well. Both bodies of freshwater are long, deep, narrow, and cold. Both lakes have an underwater wave, a *seiche*, that can throw debris from the bottom of the lake to the surface, which might explain some bizarre sightings. Lake Champlain is over four hundred feet deep and Loch Ness is seven hundred to one thousand feet in some areas. Both have a large supply of fish that these creatures could live off and not only survive but thrive. Both Champ and Nessie are said to be cryptids, creatures whose existence has been suggested but is highly unlikely, and that are still unrecognized by scientific consensus.

Cryptozoologists defend the research trying to prove that these creatures exist. They state that even "the inventory of large animals is incomplete," and that large marine creatures once thought to be extinct are later found to exist. According to the National Ocean

Service, as of January 2009, only five percent of the ocean has been explored. Since the ocean is twice as big as all the continents combined, it's easy to see how a few sea creatures could remain MIA. For example, in 1938 somebody discovered a living Coelacanth, a lobed armored fish that populated the seas sixty-four million years ago and was thought to be extinct. Since then, more than a dozen Coelacanths have beached or been caught. And let's not forget that the mountain gorilla, which was thought to be a creature of folklore until its existence was confirmed in 1902, is an example of a cryptid. Also, both the megamouth shark of Oahu, Hawaii, discovered in 1976, and the Hoan Kiem turtle, whose existence was proven in 2002, were thought to be fictitious creatures until they were discovered. The Guadalupe fur seal, thought to be extinct in 1892, was found alive in 2010. In 2018 alone there were over fifteen discoveries of new creatures, including the two headed sea slug that is both male and female, a pink grasshopper, a silver boa constrictor snake found only on Conception Island, a Ghost Octopus found two and a half miles down in the deep sea near Hawaii, and the Hammerhead bat aka Horse-bat, that some believe may have been the mistaken identity for the New Jersey Devil all these years. There are thousands of things we still don't know about our Earth, so it's not so inconceivable that a Champ-like creature may exist.

Each cryptid legend, however, starts somewhere. The tale of the Lake Champlain monster began with two Native American Indian tribes that lived along the lake, the Iroquois and the Abenaki. Both tribes had stories of a horned serpent that lived within the lake's waters. The Abenaki called the sea creature Tatoskok. Legends of the creature were passed on from generation to generation.

In 1609 a creature was supposedly spotted in the lake by the French explorer and founder of Quebec, Samuel de Champlain. Champlain, whom the lake was named after, was said to have seen Iroquois Indians fighting a monster on the bank of the lake. It was later thought that the creature Champlain described was probably a large garfish. On July 24, 1819, an article in the *Plattsburgh Republican* recorded another sighting. The paper printed an account of a Captain Crum, who said he spotted an "enormous serpentine monster" from his scow in Bulwagga Bay, New York, near Port Henry.

Apparently the creature was camera shy. It wasn't until fifty-four years later, in 1873, that another sighting was reported, first in the *Whitehall Times* and then in the *New York Times*. A railroad crew employed by the New York and Canada Railroad was working near the lake at Dresden, just north of Whitehall in Washington County in the Champlain Valley. The workers said they saw the head of an "enormous serpent" emerge from the water from the opposite shore and come toward them. They ran and the creature headed toward open water. The crew described the scene to reporters: "As he rapidly swam away, portions of his body, which seemed to be covered with bright silver like scales, glistened in the sun like burnished metal. From his nostrils he would occasionally spurt streams of water above his head to an altitude of about twenty feet. The appearance of his head was round and flat . . . his eyes were small and piercing, his mouth broad and provided with two rows of teeth." He apparently displayed these to the stunned workers. "He swam away at about ten miles an hour, and his tail which resembled that of a fish, was thrown out of the water quite often."

The workmen feared for their lives and prayed that someone would catch the beast.

A few days later, General David Barrett of Dresden and several other farmers reported lost calves, sheep, and fowl. Giant tracks nearby indicated that a heavy beast had dragged their livestock to the shoreline and reports of "great bellowings" were heard at night. Indigestion? Who's to say? Maybe it was just the rumbling of a well-fed serpent.

The Dresden area was full of marshes and caves, a perfect hiding spot for a would-be monster. According to local legend, the Chapman farm near Barrett's area had one particularly huge cave supposed to be inhabited by large monsters and reptiles. Many locals admitted to knowledge of "immense serpents in the area for over fifteen years."

A few days after the disappearance of his calves, General Barrett lost three dogs, which were found dead and mangled in the marshes. A few days after that, the *New York Times* of July 30, 1873, reported "a horse in Dresden was found with a broken back, and an ox was taken from a farm without of trace of its whereabouts." This was one hungry beast, who apparently was not water bound.

General Barrett formed a posse; the monster banquet had to stop. Armed with guns the posse tried to capture the beast, but no one was successful. Farmers were panicked at the loss of their livestock and were petitioning for aid.

Panic reached an all-time high when in August of that same year, a small steamboat, the *W. B. Eddy,* which was loaded with tourists, apparently hit the creature and nearly turned over. According to passengers' eyewitness accounts, the head and neck of the animal were seen about a hundred feet from the ship.

A writer for the *Putnam Reader* told the story of how famed showman P. T. Barnum had supposedly sent a hunter along with a guide and attendant to one of the largest caves, in order to capture a specimen of the creature for Barnum's exhibit. The writer stated that "agonizing screams were heard from the hunter inside the cave," and the guide and attendant who had accompanied him, rowed away as fast as they could, leaving the hunter to fend for himself. The hunter was never seen again.

By August 4, 1873, the *Whitehall Times* reported that the citizens of Whitehall were terrified of this monster. Other local papers goaded the editor of the *Times,* William A. Wilkins, to form a party of monster hunters to track the beast. Knowing that a capture would make good headlines, Wilkins did just that on August 9, 1873. He commandeered a steamboat, the *Molyneaux,* and his party tracked the beast to a den in Axehelve Bay, Whitehall. They had fired several shots from the deck of the ship into the cave, when they heard a low, "unearthly noise"; the beast came after them in hot pursuit. They kept firing and the order was made to go full steam ahead. As they headed downstream, the beast gained on them. Soon the infuriated beast was only twenty-five feet from their vessel. General Barrett, who was a member of the party, and the others kept firing and soon the beast was spouting blood from its head. The serpent gave one last "spasmodic twist" and slipped into the water, leaving nothing but a bloody trail. The townspeople were relieved at last. The monster was dead.

But what good is a dead monster if you can't prove it with a body? They tried to hook the submerged monster's carcass and bring it up out of the water. Unfortunately, all efforts were futile. Seizing the moment, P. T. Barnum offered a $50,000 reward for the remains of Champ, which he wanted to display in his "Mammoth World's Fair Show." Many groups and individuals searched for months, but no carcass was found.

For ten years there was no word of the beast. Then on July 31, 1883, it reared its ugly head again. The *Plattsburgh Morning Telegram* ran the following story: At 4:30 p.m. on a wild rainy day with rough seas and high winds, a break in the storm came and as the waves calmed and the sun appeared, a Clinton County sheriff named Nathan H. Mooney said he saw a creature fifty yards from him, so close he was able to see "round white spots inside its mouth." He described his encounter as follows: "I looked off to the northwest and I saw it appear again about 20 rods from us. I then discovered that it was an enormous snake or water serpent. It stood out about five feet from the water, with a long jaw, a snake-shaped head at least eight inches across at the top or flat part, and ten inches from the top of the head to the end of the jaw . . . its body, which must have been twenty-five or thirty-feet in length was pointed to the north."

After the sheriff went public with his account, others came forward with their own Champ fish tales. Whether it was a case of people jumping on the serpent bandwagon or actually seeing good ole Champ (or its now fully grown offspring) is not known. Just as the number of stories was at its highest, however, they suddenly stopped. During 1884 and 1885, the monster apparently decided to vacation in other bodies of water. The Lake Champlain monster was spotted in the Atlantic off of Massachusetts, in the Gulf of St. Lawrence, at Iberville, Quebec, in the Hudson River, and in the Atlantic Ocean off of Maine. He wasn't carrying a suitcase.

In the summer of 1886, satisfied with his two-year exploration, Champ returned with an appetite for attention. The *Morning Telegram* printed a Vermont fisherman's description of Champ. "He was sporting and snorting in the morning sun. His body was out of the water about fourteen feet, his head was well up, and his great, red tongue kept licking his chops as if expecting a breakfast of some healthy camper; his eyes, as big as powder kegs, glowed wildly, his teeth looked like polished steel, and his horns were bright and brass-mounted; a kind of whalebone mane ran down his neck and a big buzz saw ornamented his breast. Scales as big as milk pails ornamented his sides, and his nickel-plated tail was flailing in the air for bald eagles. His color was a handsome drab with white points, and his belly was old gold."

That year almost daily sightings, not all so far-fetched, were reported in the paper. These stories were not told by the local drunkards, but by men of prestige, doctors, businessmen, navigators, clergymen, and salesmen. The creature was seen in every part of the lake from north to south, east to west, in shallow or deep water. People saw it swimming, diving, floating, and frolicking, and it was described as everything from a large Newfoundland dog to a log.

People shot at it, threw stones at it, chased it, and tried to hook it with fishing lines. In two stories the creature was caught and got away. The *Plattsburgh Sentinel* offered a $1,000 reward for its capture, dead or alive, with the provision it had to be over twenty feet in length.

On Friday May 13, 1887, however, a well-known sportsman and writer, "Adirondack Murray," said he had solved the Champ mystery. A large crowd of people gathered at Battery Park in Burlington, Vermont, was viewing the monster, which had apparently been showing off for almost three hours in the bay near Juniper Island just three miles away from the Burlington shore. Murray said onlookers watched with the naked eye. The creature seemed to be brown and about a hundred feet longer than expected. He said, "His speed was astonishing." The sea serpent disappeared for a few minutes and Murray ran and got some high-powered field glasses. When the creature popped his head up again, Murray was shocked to see that it was not some giant sea serpent but a flock of hundreds of plovers. The lighthouse keeper on Juniper Island, who was nearer the spectacle, confirmed Murray's observation. The *Sentinel* ran Murray's explanation but other papers refused to believe his story. No one wanted the legend of Champ to die, so it lived on.

On May 16, 1887, the *Morning Telegram* reported that a party of soldiers was fishing off the Garrison and caught a sea creature, half fish, half animal, about fourteen inches in length with a "flat arrow shaped head, four legs, tufted and shaped like an eel." It was said to be the offspring of the sea lizard and the paper suggested that a "brood of these vipers was being hatched in Lake Champlain."

Sightings of Champ continued, and on occasion, he would wander into other lakes. In the summer of 1904, there were multiple sightings of Champ in Lake George. Years later in the 1960s, however, the Champ in Lake George was proven to be an imposter, a "sea monster" operated by pulleys that was built for a prank by local artist Henry Watrous and his chauffeur. Watrous believed that some clever Scotsmen were doing the same thing in Loch Ness. After its debut at a celebrity party on the lake, the creature made cameo appearances for the rest of the summer. In 1962, the mechanical creature was discovered by a Glenns Falls photographer. Since 1971, it has been on display at the Lake George Institute of History and Art.

Whether real or not, Champ still brings tourism to Vermont; Port Henry, New York; and Lake Champlain to this day. To protect tourism and the creature, on April 20, 1982, the Vermont House of Representatives passed Resolution H.R. 19, protecting Champ "from any willful act resulting in death, injury or harassment." The same year, the New York State Assembly passed a similar resolution. But it wasn't only the law that kept the legend of Champ alive.

In 2003, the Fauna Communications Research Institute, working in conjunction with the Discovery Channel, used echolocation to see if it could detect the monster. It recorded the sounds of a large unknown creature, one that the researchers could only say sounded closest to a beluga whale or an orca.

A large creature comes with a large appetite. In 2008, three government agencies, the US Fish and Wildlife Service, the New York Department of Environmental Conservation, and the Vermont Department of Fish and Wildlife, noticed an inexplicable fluctuation in the levels of certain breeds of fish. Although there are cycles in all animals' mating and herd size, this was a sudden change, which they attributed to an unknown X-Factor. When the public heard this report, they said it was Champ, their friendly local lake monster having a snack. The government agencies refused to jump to the same conclusion.

On the other side of the world in the Scottish Highlands, on June 20, 1975, at 4:32 a.m., underwater films of Nessie, the Loch Ness Monster, were taken by the Academy of Applied Sciences from Boston, Massachusetts. The films were said to have shown that Nessie was twenty-five feet in length. As a result of the films, Nessie has now been classified by the International Union for Conservation of Nature (IUCN) as an endangered species known as *Nessiteras rhombopteryx,* although its actual existence has yet to be proven. If Nessie has that classification, why not Champ? Today, Joseph W. Zarzynski, one of the foremost authorities on USOs (unidentified swimming objects), has made trips to Scotland to compare beasts and he is determined to get Champ classified as well.

Lake Champlain was at one time part of the Atlantic Ocean. Glacial melting filled the "Champlain Valley," forming "Lake Vermont," the granddaddy of today's Lake Champlain. When the great ice barrier melted, seawater flowed through, forming the Champlain seas, which ran through Port Henry and Whitehall. Then the flow of water reversed and salt water flowed out of Lake Champlain. There is evidence that the lake was once sea-based; the remains of walruses, seals, and whales have been found in the lake. Champ could have originated in the Atlantic Ocean.

On February 22, 2006, ABC News ran a segment titled "Is there a monster in Lake Champlain?" Film footage showed an odd wake. Gerald Richards, a forensic image analyst, said, after examining the film, "I can't find anything in there that would suggest or indicate to me that this has been fabricated or manipulated in any way. However, there's no place in there that I can actually see an animal or any other object on the surface."

As recently at October of 2015, Cindy (last name unknown) reported she was snorkeling along the shore of Lake Champlain and captured underwater footage of Champ. She claims he clamped onto her arm for a few seconds and then let her go. (Maybe she wasn't his brand of tasty, or maybe it was just a warning that he is tired of having his picture taken.) The video was sent to the YouTube channel "Thirdphaseofmoon." Many other Champ videos have surfaced online as well. There seems to be no shortage of accounts. But do all these people need glasses or therapy?

As you enter the town of Port Henry, New York, you will see this sign, which lists all citizens past and present who have claimed to see the sea monster known as Champ. Every year on the first Saturday of August, Port Henry holds a Champ Day celebration.

Is Champ just a legend or is he an evasive, unnamed prehistoric beast who really does exist? We know for sure that today's Champ is a loved and celebrated creature. Unlike the Champ of long ago, the contemporary Champ appears docile and does not ravage towns or chase workers. On the first Saturday of every August, the village of Port Henry, New York, has a Champ Day festival with vendors, local authors, music, and a Champ float. On the edge of town stands a large sign that reads CHAMP SIGHTINGS IN BULWAGGA BAY AREA. The sign proudly lists the names of all 133 people, from 1609 to 1990, who have been lucky enough to have a gander at the creature in this area.

Whether Champ is a zeuglodon, a plesiosaur, a seiche wave, a giant lake sturgeon, or just a bump on a log, one thing remains certain: People living near or visiting Lake Champlain should always have their cameras poised and ready as they will continue to see things in the water and wonder what they might be. And if they have something on camera, their story will at least be more than just another fishy tale.

CHAPTER 8

Bizarre Tales of Buckout Road

Westchester County is known as an upscale place filled with doctors, lawyers, and businessmen who live in beautifully adorned houses with manicured lawns. But there is a part of Westchester that it would be smart to avoid, especially at night. That area is Buckout Road, aka Head Road, a woodsy, desolate, one-lane back road that connects the eastern part of White Plains to West Harrison, New York, in Westchester County. Most of this one-and-a-quarter-mile road is located in the village of Harrison, just twenty-seven miles from midtown Manhattan. Up until a few years ago, the road didn't even have streetlights.

The road sends shivers up the spines of all who know it. Its dark history begins in the 1600s and is filled with stories of Native American scalpings, mystical animals, Revolutionary War battles, murders, a hanging, a serial killer, a slave cemetery, grave robbing, and arson. In addition, the road is home to every kind of urban legend imaginable, from paranormal activity to witches, haunted mansions, possessed lawn ornaments, and flesh-eating albinos.

How did Buckout Road gain its reputation? Answers to this question are intertwined with the history of the area. The town of Harrison, New York, was originally inhabited by a tribe of Native Americans known as the Siwanoy. When Dutch settlers moved into the area to trade in the 1600s, there was tension between the Native Americans and Europeans. Four main families settled in the area. One of these was the family of Captain John Buckhout (yes that's Buckhout with the "H"), who settled near the Hudson River and established a farm.

Tension between the two peoples led to battles, and in 1643, the settlers launched attacks on the Indians, butchering many of them. The Siwanoys countered with an attack that destroyed a Dutch settlement in nearby Pelham Bay. Another attack by the settlers in 1644 practically wiped out the tribe and put an end to the battles. A peace treaty was signed between the Dutch and the Native American tribes in the Hudson Valley area on August 30, 1645.

In 1695 the Native American tribes sold their land to John Harrison, a Long Island Quaker. According to local legend, Harrison was given twenty-four hours to ride his horse around an area that would become his. Eventually, more than seventeen miles of land was officially recognized as the town of Harrison by New York State on March 7, 1788. The Siwanoy tribe eventually disappeared from the area, but the earliest legend of Buckout Road had its origins with these people.

THE GREAT WHITE DEER

The Siwanoy tribe believed that during the full moon a beautiful Great White Deer visited Buckout Road. Some say it was a "ghost deer." This deer would bring great fortune to all who lay eyes on it. The legend spread to neighboring tribes and people would travel from the Great Lakes to catch a glimpse of it and receive whatever

The Siwanoy tribe believed that during the full moon a beautiful Great White Deer visited Buckout Road. Some referred to it as the "ghost deer." Native American Indians would travel from miles around to catch a glimpse of this deer. It turns out there is a protected herd of white deer living in Seneca Falls, New York, at an abandoned army depot. The author herself captured a photo of one, nesting in the woods, but there are many photos of these beautiful deer online. The Seneca white deer are leucistic, meaning they lack all pigmentation in the hair, but have normal brown-colored eyes. Albino deer, which lack only the pigment melanin, have pink eyes and are extremely rare.

fortune the Great White Deer would bestow. One Native American known as "Indian Dan" was religious in his journey. Every year from 1805 to 1866, he would travel to the Buckout Road area in hopes of seeing the Great White One. A street near Buckout Road was named White Deer Lane in tribute to this "legend". However, it turns out this legend is actually true! While white deer no longer reside in Westchester (the rents are too high), there is actually a protected herd of white deer (not albino deer) living in abundance in an abandoned army depot in Seneca Falls, New York. As of 2018 tours have been started to support the herd of white leucistic deer (meaning they lack all pigmentation in the hair, but have the normal brown-colored eyes) for curious onlookers to try to spot these beautiful creatures that the Siwanoy spoke of long ago.)

GHOSTS IN OLD AND SACRED BURIAL GROUNDS

Harrison sold his land in 1727 to a group of Quakers who promptly built a meetinghouse on Buckout Road. The Quakers, who were nonviolent, did not believe in slavery. They freed their African-American slaves between 1773 and 1783, long before the law freeing Northern slaves was decreed on July 4, 1827.

To help their freed slaves earn a living, the Quakers gave them farmland to work on Stony Hill, which was on Buckout Road as well. This area became the single largest African-American area in Westchester County.

Six-and-a-half acres of land in the woods off of Buckout Road were allotted to the freed slaves as Stony Hill Cemetery, the sight of legendary supernatural activity. It holds the remains of over two hundred freed slaves as well as black war veterans. Today it is conjectured that the cemetery was built on top of sacred Native American burial grounds. Many ghostly figures have been spotted in the cemetery, ranging from angry, displaced Indians to Dutch children and soldiers. So much blood has been shed in the area that it's hard to tell which ghosts are the most disturbed. Photos taken there catch orbs of light; numerous recent blogs have been written about ghostly encounters. The ghost most often seen is a black woman dressed in white, dancing, they say, to the beat of drums heard in the distance.

THE LEGENDARY BATTLE OF WHITE PLAINS

In 1776 the Revolutionary War encroached on Buckout Road. It seems that General Washington had battles everywhere, and the Horton Grist Mill off of Lake Street, a stone's throw from Buckout Road, was the setting for the two-day battle of White Plains on October 28, 1776. The Redcoats wanted Washington's ammunition, which was stored in the mill. Forty-seven casualties of the battle added to the bloodshed in the area. The British won this round; after the battle, British and Hessian soldiers camped on a nearby tenant farm in Irvington, owned by Captain John Buckhout; they used the farm as a stakeout during the rest of the war.

THE WHITE LADY, OR THE GHOST OF MARY BUCKHOUT

The Buckhouts, who settled in the area in the 1600s, were a prominent family in Westchester. One family member, Mary Buckhout, supposedly lived on Buckout Road across the street from the family cemetery, where one version of the story has it that she saw grave robbers at work. The robbers murdered her to eliminate the witness to their crime. Another version of the story has it that she hanged herself from a tree near the Buckhout mansion. Whether she was murdered or committed suicide, she is said to haunt Buckout Road dressed in white.

One Buckout resident swears that on several occasions the French doors leading to his outside porch, which faces the woods, have flown open on their own, even after he has locked them himself. As soon as the doors open, an apparition of a woman dressed in white swooshes past him. Others claim to have spotted the White Lady on Buckout Road as they have been driving at night.

Many stories have been told of grave robbers who came to Buckout Road cemeteries, dug up the graves of prestigious families, leaving only open coffins. A number of the robbers were said to have dug up the bones for satanic rituals. News of these thefts often made the local papers. One story concerned Mary Buckhout, whose grave had been dug up and her body stolen. It is said that her ghost roams the countryside looking for the vandals who did it. Those who are brave enough to go into the cemeteries at night claim to have felt her hand on their shoulders. Apparently, one of Mary's most common ghostly traits is reaching out to touch someone.

THE CAPTIVE SLAVES AND A MYSTERIOUS POOL OF BLOOD

This event is supposed to have occurred during the late 1800s. The story goes that the Buckhouts were holding a group of albino slaves captive at a nearby farm. The youngest Buckhout daughter was angry with her family for doing this. One dark, rainy, thunderous night the daughter went mad, freed the slaves, and killed her family. In remorse, she hanged herself. News spread and a manhunt for the albino slaves ensued. Three of the freed slaves murdered another family. When they were caught, they were hanged from a tree branch in front of the Buckhout's home, and their bodies were gutted. The blood from the bodies formed a pool beneath them. Legend has it that to this very day, "wet spots" appear no matter what the weather on the ground beneath where they were hanged.

THE LAST MAN HANGED IN WHITE PLAINS

Another member of the Buckhout family, Isaac Buckhout, was an influential man, a local magistrate of sorts. According to the book *Eight Who Were Hanged,* on New Year's Day in 1870, Isaac decided to have a little get-together. He invited his neighbor, Alfred Rendell, and Rendell's son for dinner. While his wife, Louisa Ann, was serving dinner, Isaac excused himself for a moment and came back with a double-barreled shotgun. He served up a healthy portion of lead to Alfred and killed him. He then shot Alfred's son and crushed his wife's skull with the gun. He had suspected that his wife had been cheating on him and he figured this was the best way to handle it. According to another source, he left his home, walked a little over twelve miles to the nearby village of Tarrytown, sat down in a pub, and started to drink. He sat there until the sheriff tracked him down and arrested him. Three trials were held, one for each victim. The jury deliberated for days over his sentence, and in the end, he was convicted of murder and hanged. He was the last man to be hanged in White Plains. Louisa Ann is said to still haunt their property.

A CURSED FARM

James Foster purchased land in 1823 located at 500 Hall Avenue. Hall Avenue turns into Buckout Road. The Underground Railroad would later run through part of this land. Three generations of Fosters lived on the property; in 1971, the farm, now owned by the Baldwins, was the target of arson. Two of the barns were burned to the ground, horses were injured, and one eyewitness saw a charred cow roaming the farm with its side exposed for days before it died.

The last Baldwin farmer who lived on the property was severely mentally ill and would often curse the local children and talk to himself. His house had no furniture, but was filled with "weird geometric drawings." He was found dead on his porch in 1979 by a local White Plains Eastview Junior High School student, appropriately named Wayne Slaughter. The body was found in an unusual position: Baldwin was face up with his hands spread out in a cross-like fashion. The farmer's eyes were gouged out. For years locals said they would see ghostly figures in the upper windows of the farmhouse. In August of 1982, the farm burned to the ground, once again the target of arson.

Eric Pleska, one of the leading authorities on the mysteries of Buckout Road, had his own encounter with the ghostly farmer during his high school years. He and a friend went to shoot a video in the nearby cemetery. His mother was filming. At one point, the boys were about to turn and run, when all of a sudden a farmer in overalls stood in front of them holding a pitchfork. Both of the boys were startled and asked the man what was the matter. He pointed, then disappeared. When they reviewed the tape, they could see themselves talking on the film, but the farmer was not there. Eric was so fascinated with this he made it his mission to explore the legends and created a website called www.bedofnailz.com.

The city of White Plains, which now owns the farmland, has turned it into The Baldwin Farm Community Gardens Recreation & Parks, where individuals can buy plots for cultivation. If you go there, you will see a sign that says GARDENERS ONLY.

THE BOOGEYMAN AND THE
CASE OF THE HANGING BOYFRIEND

If you were going to wish that one of the legends of Buckout Road had no basis in truth, this would be the one. The legend is about a villain of the worst kind, a child-eating cannibal serial killer. Hamilton Howard Albert Fish (1870–1936) was a child rapist and cannibal who boasted he had "had children in every state." His crimes were so hideous he was given several nicknames, the *Gray Man,* the *Werewolf of Wisteria,* the *Boogeyman,* and the *Brooklyn Vampire.* He came from a mentally ill family; at the age of twelve he had a homosexual relationship. He later became a male prostitute. Despite his homosexual tendencies, he married and had six children. Even so, he would still molest boys under the age of six. Fish began to hear voices and said that "John the Apostle" had told him to inflict self-harm, so he beat himself with a nail-studded paddle. On hearing about a famine in China in which some people would kidnap and kill young children for meat, Fish developed a taste for human flesh.

He would choke his victims to death, cut off their heads, and use a meat clever, a butcher knife, and a saw to chop them up and cook them. Fish said he raped, killed, and ate around one hundred people, mostly children, between 1924 and 1932. In 1934 he was captured and put on trial for the kidnapping and murder of Grace Budd. He took her to an abandoned home, Wisteria Cottage, in a place called Worthington Woods in Westchester County. The trial took place in 1935 in White Plains. It only took ten days to convict him; the jury found him sane and guilty. Before his execution, he said that electrocution would be the "supreme thrill of my life." He was executed by electric chair in Sing Sing prison on January 16, 1936. At sixty-five, he was the oldest man ever executed at the prison.

Supposedly, many years later, on a rainy night in the 1970s, a boy and girl were driving on Buckout Road when their car battery died. The boy knocked on the door of the nearest house for help while the girl waited inside the car. Several minutes later, the girl-friend heard three distinct thumps on the roof of the car. She slowly got out of the car to see what the noise was. Horrified, she saw her boyfriend hanging from a tree, his neck snapped and his feet banging against the hood of the car. The boy had knocked on the door of a house that had belonged to none other than the cannibal killer, Albert Fish. Apparently, even death could not stop his thirst for murder. While the Albert Fish murders really happened, the hanging boy story remains an urban legend that has been reported to have happened in many parts of New York.

The Haunted Mansion and the Slaughterhouses

The Buckhouts owned a grand, gated estate on Buckout Road that included a main mansion, a farmhouse, and a road that led to several pig slaughterhouses.

In 2002, the family who bought the house was using it as an office for their fuel company. One of the sons, Pete, says the house had a "creepy feel to it" and, in one instance, he found neckties "from another century" on the doorknobs. Photos of the mansion would show ghostly orbs shining around it.

Beside the Buckhout murders, others happened in the mansion as well. One story tells of a babysitter working at the mansion who kept getting strange phone calls. She called the police, who told her the calls were coming from inside the house. Later she found the children murdered. This incident was the inspiration for the movie *When a Stranger Calls*. The mansion was torn down in 2003. A new home now takes its place, located at the end of Old Carriage House Road, just off of Buckout Road. If you stop in front of the slaughterhouses, some say you can still hear chopping and banging noises.

The Buckhout family cemetery on Hall Avenue has been renovated as well. Up until the early 1970s, it was overgrown with shrubs and broken tombstones. Although there are forty-three bodies buried on the land, there has been so much vandalism that today only one stone remains in the family cemetery. Even that has been chipped on the upper right-hand corner by vandals. The solitary tombstone reads:

JOHN BUCKHOUT MARCH 12, 1847 TO FEB. 6, 1915

CHARLOTTE COWAN—

HIS WIFE DEC. 30, 1851 TO MAY 15, 1927

HAUNTED LAWN ORNAMENTS

Another Buckout Road legend originated in the late 1990s. It concerns a house that had two greyhound dog statues on the property. As the story goes, one of the dogs would come to life at night. In some versions, the dog is evil, a Hound of the Baskervilles type;

John Buckhout's tombstone is the only one left in the family cemetery on the road that bears the family name. The graveyard has been vandalized so many times that even this remaining stone has been damaged. The family plot is located in Harrison, New York, in Westchester County, on Hall Avenue, which turns into Buckout Road.
PHOTO COURTESY OF D.V. KILIAN

another version contends that the dog is protecting the family from the multitude of creepy things in the area.

One young man named Ryan relates an incident in which he took his girlfriend to the house one night because she wanted to see the statues. They focused their flashlights on the statues, but nothing peculiar happened. Since Buckout Road is a dead end, they drove to the end of it, turned around, and went by again to check out the statues once more. This time, they noticed that one of the pedestals was empty. They looked to see if the statue had fallen over, but there was no sign of it. At that moment, somewhere in the distance, they heard a dog bark. They got in the car and quickly drove away, never to return.

MARY'S LANTERN

Another haunted lawn ornament story, famous for decades, is the legend of Mary's Lantern. One of the houses on Buckout Road displayed a statue of Mother Mary. The story goes that if the lantern was lit, it was safe to venture forth; if it was not lit, potential danger lay ahead in the form of evil ghosts and goblins. In another variation, Mary was not only holding a lantern, but was also seen crying. Sometimes tears, sometimes blood ran down her face. There are those who claim that the blood was some form of stigmata. (This author, who believes in Mother Mary, feels maybe she was just upset because she was holding that lantern for so darn long!)

THREE XS AND THE WITCHES

We've all heard the expression *X* marks the spot. In the case of Buckout Road, three red, spray-painted *X*s caused all the problems. These three *X*s were said to be located where Buckout Road turns into Hall Avenue. Back in the 1600s, this site was on the crest of a hill overlooking the Buckhout/Baldwin/Foster family cemetery.

There are two versions of the story. The first is that the *X*s marked the spot where three women accused of being witches in the 1600s were burned at the stake. Unfortunately, there seems to be no record of three women burned at the stake in this area. Local legend had it, though, that if you drove over the *X*s, your car would stall on the spot and "strange things would happen" for no apparent reason.

The second version claimed that the *X*s marked where the witches were buried. Their supernatural powers rose from beyond the grave and killed the car batteries.

As if the *X*s weren't enough of an indicator of black magic, a rope that hung from a tree standing over the *X*s was said to have been affected by their powers as well. The very rope that was used to hang the magical trio, it could not be pulled, broken, cut, or burned, and hung there for centuries. Apparently, however, the spell has been broken, since neither the *X*s nor the rope remains. A local resident, Joe, says he was told that the *X*s were for aerial identification purposes, for what he was not sure. The hill has been leveled out and the street widened. The *X*s have been paved over and are now just a vague memory from the past.

THE FLESH-EATING ALBINOS

One last meaning of the *X*s also gave the road its unofficial name, Head Road. They were said to serve as a warning to would-be travelers about a certain red house in West Harrison on Buckout Road, a house said to be inhabited by a gang of flesh-eating albinos. The story has it that if you stopped in front of the house and honked three times, the white-faced gang would come out and try to eat you. If they weren't in flesh-eating mode, they would just chase you. The more these stories spread, the more people would come up with ways to "test" the albinos. One way was to stand in front of their house and curse the leader of the albino clan whose name was Moses. If you yelled profanity, red eyes would stare from the windows or from the surrounding woods. Others claimed you would hear voices right next to you, even though no physical bodies were around.

Joe, the present owner of Moses's home on Buckout Road, says that Moses was not an albino but did have long white hair. He had two sons, one of whom was albino. One of Moses's sons was found dead in a car on Buckout Road; he had committed suicide. Moses, grieving at his son's death and angered at constantly being harassed by the local teens, would run out and chase them, which helped perpetuate the myth.

The harassment got bad. One night a teen pulled up outside the house planning to place an M-80 in the mailbox. When he opened the mailbox, a child's decapitated head fell out and landed at his feet. The nickname Head Road stuck after that. Needless to say, if the story has any shred of truth to it, the teen learned not to mess with Moses and his family again.

All of these legends created a terrifying experience on Buckout Road that served as a kind of rite of passage for teenagers. Indeed, Joe said many teenagers would be dropped in front of his house at night. When questioned, they said they were there to "survive" the night.

Other homeowners in the area would try to scare the teens away. One blogpost dated August 9, 2010, written by a resident on Buckout Road, reads, "We'd hide behind the stone wall where the cemetery was and scare people. As for the albinos, there was a family but they were the nicest people ever. . . . We would hangout [sic] on that road and scare the kids that thought the area was haunted. So there were albinos but just bad stories linked to them."

Unfortunately, the original red house where the albino family lived was partially burned down and Joe, the present owner, revamped, rebuilt, and extended it.

The legends of Buckout Road still haunt Harrison today, even though much of the area was developed in the late 1990s and is now filled with sprawling mansions, and a good section of the road on Old Lake Street is a paved two-lane thoroughfare. There is a stretch of road, however, where the yellow dividing line vanishes and it dwindles into a one-lane, barely passable strip of asphalt. At this spot on Buckout Road, the creepiness of haunted cemeteries and abandoned buildings begins. No matter how brightly lit the other areas of Buckout Road are, the light cannot erase the centuries of mystery, both real and fictional, that surround it.

And while the majority of the residents would like these legends to die so they can live in peace, apparently, others feel differently. In 2011, one former New Rochelle resident, John Pascucci, wrote a screenplay that was picked up by Ambush Entertainment about the Buckout Road legends, with 90210 actor and director Jason Priestly set to be on board. Ultimately, it became a Trimuse Entertainment film directed by Matthew Curie Holmes and released (based on the Pascucci screenplay) at the Calgary International Film Festival in Canada on November 24, 2017, called *Buckout Road*. The film starred actress Dominique Provost-Chalkley (*Avengers* and *Wynonna Earp*) and actor Danny Glover, and won fourteen awards. So, unfortunately, the residents of Buckout Road will have to buck up and accept that their infamous road will forever be etched in the minds of curiosity seekers as one of the most fascinating haunts to visit in all of Westchester.

CHAPTER 9

McGurk's Suicide Bar

When John McGurk came to New York in 1870 at the tender age of seventeen, he had one thing on his mind—making money. He wanted to be the best at something. Little did he know he would become the "best" by owning the worst den of iniquity ever immortalized in New York City history all because of a bizarre fad.

After a few menial jobs and a short stint in school, McGurk quickly learned whom to make friends with. By 1885 he got in with the crooked Tammany Hall crowd. He figured with them on his side he could open a series of clip joints and not be bothered by the law. He chose the area of the Bowery to establish himself. The Bowery at that time was a main road that led from the lower to the upper parts of Manhattan.

In the 1890s, prostitution and gambling were creeping their way up from Water Street to the Bowery. The Bowery now had the largest number of flophouses, brothels, rigged auctions, fleshpot establishments, pawnbrokers, dime museums, fortune-telling agencies, thief's markets, tattoo parlors, and fire sales in the city. It was also home to low-class theaters, where it wasn't uncommon for prostitutes to peddle their wares in the top balconies while plays were in session. In addition to that fabulous lineup of establishments, the Bowery also boasted groggeries, aka taverns or saloons, with names like *Tub of Blood*, *The Morgue*, and *Hells Gate*. Seventeen of these taverns were on the east and sixty-five of them on the west side of the Bowery. The Bowery is the only major thoroughfare in New York City never to have had a single church built on it, and rightfully so.

Other than the sailors, the main clientele in these areas was not exactly made up of the upstanding citizens of society; it consisted of pickpockets, panhandlers, gang members, morphine addicts, and prostitutes. McGurk, in hopes of attracting the sea-bound crowd, opened three establishments with names like *The Mug*, *Sailors Snug Harbor*, and *The Merrimac* on Third Avenue. Unfortunately, Mayor Hewitt did not care about McGurk's connections and these places became targets of police raids and were closed down for encouraging "inappropriate behavior."

Being persistent and believing in the American Dream, McGurk tried again. In 1895 he had his eye on a five-story brick tenement building that was originally a hotel for returning Civil War soldiers. It was located on the east side, at 295 Bowery Street, just above Houston Street in the heart of the "Old Red Light District," which was perfect for his type of clientele. This time he simply called the place McGurk's Saloon.

McGurk wanted his saloon to stick out, so he became the first person in New York City to use an electric sign. This bright sign caught the locals' attention from blocks away. It also caught the eyes of the sailors, and since he already had a reputation among the sea-men, they knew this was the place for drinks and "delight." It was said that McGurk's "business card reached every seaport in the world."

As soon as you walked into McGurk's, you were greeted by a deep dark interior. There were separate entrances for men and women. The men had a direct entry to the bar, and the women could reach it via a long corridor on the side. There was also a large back room.

To make sure that his establishment ran smoothly, McGurk had to hire the "right" people to handle his unsavory crowd. His staff consisted of the following shady characters:

Charles Steele, aka "Short-Change Charley," was the head-waiter. Short-Change's claim to fame was that he was once arrested for burglary and attempted murder. But "lucky" for him, none of the witnesses at the scene could identify him, and so here he was working at this "fine" establishment.

Bart O'Connor was the manager. Bart had been arrested for "illegal registration." In other words, he was trying to buy votes for the Tammany Hall politicians by offering men free lodging and drinks in exchange. Along the same lines, one of the bounc-ers, John Sullivan, aka Charles Moon, was also working on the illegal voting scam ticket. He had spent two-and-a-half years in Sing Sing for it. Another of his upstanding employees was Com-modore Dutch. He chaired a "society" that would collect funds for charity. The only problem was the charity was for one person only—himself. This con artist spent forty years behind bars after he worked at McGurk's.

And last but not least was his bouncer extraordinaire, "Eat 'Em Up Jack" McManus. McGurk claimed another first with McManus; he was the first bouncer on record ever hired in a public place. McManus was a huge former prizefighter with cauliflower ears and a beat-up, pock-marked face to match. At the time, he was the right-hand man to Paul Kelly, the leader of the notorious Five Points Gang. McManus loved to dress in fine clothes. His official title at McGurk's was "sheriff" and he was armed. One of his jobs was to enforce the house rules. For example, if he saw anyone stealing, he was allowed to do spot searches. If customers protested or annoyed him in any way, he'd simply punch them and the next thing they knew they were seeing cartoon birdies swirling around their heads. McManus was arrested several times, but always released because, miraculously, all of his victims would suffer amnesia and not press charges. One brave victim, however, did squeal to the police—McManus tore off his ear. The case was promptly dropped.

Now that his staff was established, McGurk had to consider entertainment, besides the lure of the prostitutes, so he hired singing waiters and a small band.

McGurk wanted to make sure his bar was making money, too. He served whiskey at five cents a glass, but to guarantee the liquor was stretched as far as it could go, it was often watered down. Now it would have been fine if the bartenders just used water, but they added another liquid as well, to give the drinks a special kick. That liquid was camphor, which at the time was used in moth repellents and as an embalming fluid. Sometimes, however, the bartenders didn't mix in the right amount and the patrons died. Oops! But this did not stop McGurk from serving up those drinks.

In addition to embalming fluid, other additives included benzene, turpentine, and cocaine sweepings and were liberally mixed in. The waiters were also known to slip new unsuspecting patrons a

Mickey Finn (chloral hydrate). This would dope them up and then they would be robbed in the back alley by the staff and, in some cases, brutally beaten. This was not an establishment for wimps!

Then there were the McGurk "girls" who would perform their nightly "duties" for the men, which, of course, made his place once again a target for police raids. The year he opened, the *New York Times* reported, "They charge McGurk with admitting minors to a concert saloon where intoxicating liquors are sold. When they visited the place the agents found it overrun with men and women of the lowest type. Everything was carried out in a disgusting manner."

During one raid, the agents found a fifteen-year-old in the midst of everything by the name of Mary Ormsby. McGurk was arrested and the juvenile taken to a room in the Gerry Society, a watchdog organization whose mission was to advocate for children in the workplace and protect them from unhealthy environments.

Mysteriously McGurk always got off; of course, his friends at Tammany Hall might have had something to do with this. McGurk was also often arrested for running a "disorderly house or brothel" but was released because of the transient nature of his "hotel" guests. Not much ever came of the raids, and so with no punishment, the charades continued.

McGurk wanted to make sure that all his patrons felt comfortable coming to his place despite the arrests, and so to give them a fighting chance to escape, he built several secret passageways for a quick exit whenever the police felt the need to make an unannounced visit. The passageways led to exits on First Street, Second Avenue, Houston Street, or to a place called Horseshoe

Alley, which was so dark, empty, and creepy that it was pitch black even on a sunny day.

But dark and empty did not only describe the escape alleys; it was also a fitting description of how the girls that worked at McGurk's felt. The Bowery was already a magnet for thousands of women and teenage girls involved in the oldest profession, prostitution. For many of them, this was the only way they knew how to make money. It was said that you would have to have fallen to the lowest of the low to sell your body at McGurk's.

One reporter, James McCabe Jr., described the type of woman who frequented McGurk's. "You would find her in the terrible dens, sailor's dance house, and living hells of some kindred locality. She is a mass of disease, utterly vile and repulsive, steadily dying from her bodily ailments, and the effects of rum and gin. She has reached the bottom of the ladder and can go no lower. She knows it, and in a sort of dumbly desperate way is glad it is so. Life is such a daily torture to her, hope has so entirely left her, that death offers her relief."

That's exactly what started to happen. Thrown into the depths of despair, many prostitutes decided to commit suicide, right there at McGurk's. This bizarre fad caught on, and one by one they would stage their deaths. Many of these girls were between the ages of sixteen and eighteen.

There were two popular methods of suicide. The first was to drink carbolic acid, or phenol. Carbolic acid was commonly used as a disinfectant and therefore easy to purchase at the local pharmacy. However, while it was easy to purchase, drinking it was not an easy way to die. The acid caused severe chemical burns when it came into contact with the skin. Ingesting it was very painful, and those who witnessed the deaths say the victims would die slowly, "writhing in agony." (To give you an example of how bad a death by carbolic acid was, the Nazis used to inject it into concentration camp victims' veins, and sometimes directly into their hearts.)

Other women who wanted to end it more quickly decided to go with the other popular suicide option, which was to leap to their death from the top floor of the attached hotel and die on impact.

Sometimes the fear of suicide made the girls nervous. But instead of trying to find a way out, they would plan to die in pairs. Such was the case with two of the McGurk prostitutes, Blond Madge Davenport and Big Mame. In October of 1899, they made a pact to off themselves at the bar at the same time by each downing a shot of the deadly liquid. So they purchased the acid at a local pharmacy. Nervously they sat at the bar, then looked at each other and toasted. Davenport downed her dose in one fell swoop and died a horrible and painful death. Big Mame tried to gulp hers down, but in her nervousness, spilled the acid, which burned and disfigured her face. She was now told she was too ugly to work at McGurk's and was banned from the place forever.

In 1899, there were six confirmed deaths and seven failed attempts. Word quickly spread and it became public knowledge that McGurk's was the place to meet your maker.

Forever the businessman, McGurk decided to "cash" in on this as a marketing idea and renamed his place "Suicide Hall." When some commented that he was callous for using people's misfortunes as a marketing ploy, he responded, "I'm just an innocent bystander." But the next time a victim killed herself, he decided to do a public eulogy. That victim was Tina Gordon. McGurk stood over her body and said, "Most of the women who come to my place have been on the downgrade too long to think of reforming . . . I just want to say that I never pushed a girl downhill any more than I ever refused a helping hand to one who wanted to climb."

The suicides in his bar were getting so commonplace that the waiters began to notice the signs. When they thought someone was going to do it, they would form a flying wedge and escort the person out on the street before the agonizing death would start.

However, by then, McGurk's business actually began to depend on the suicides as one of its morbid allures. Upper-class tourists would come to his saloon after a night at the theater and peek in or actually sit outside the place in hopes of witnessing someone plunge to her death. In a macabre way, McGurk didn't want his star attraction to stop.

By 1899 the city had had enough. Governor Theodore Roosevelt and Republican state legislators formed a committee to investigate the Tammany Hall corruption and the dens of iniquity. Leading the charge was Robert Maze, who was sick and tired of this "overt illegal activity." With the help of testimony from a teenage prostitute, Emma Hartig, who had attempted suicide in the McGurk place, he was able to build a case.

While the case was pending, the staff at McGurk's continued in their normal way. On March 11, 1900, the *New York Times* reported that as an "intoxicated patron left the bar, two men [Bartender William Strauss and McGurk's nephew, Philip McKenzie] followed him up the Bowery and attacked and robbed him at the corner of Bleecker Street." Judge Newburger, who had presided over many McGurk's tavern cases, wanted Suicide Hall to end.

The raids became more frequent. On March 23, 1901, the *Times* reported, "The place was crowded . . . dancing was going on with the rest of the amusements when the police startled everybody by rushing in. . . . Then Col. Monroe indicated the men he had warrants for, and they were placed under arrest and taken to the station house by some of the policemen. . . . The men and women in McGurk's were excited and shouted that they wanted to get out, while the crowd outside yelled, 'Back.' When the three prisoners were taken out the crowd jeered them."

The pressure was on. McGurk took his sign down, but placed a "barker" outside his place to make sure that those who came by knew it was still the same McGurk's.

The new police captain, James Churchill, told McGurk he was going down. McGurk just laughed. Churchill kept the pressure on, and eventually, McGurk nervously asked the captain to allow him a month to dispose of his lease. The captain was satisfied, feeling that McGurk was scared. In 1902 John McGurk was forced to shut down Suicide Hall.

But the last laugh was on city hall. To escape conviction on "keeping a disorderly house," McGurk pretended he was nervous and sick and didn't show up in court. Instead he had his counsel say that he was ill in a sanitarium. But it was a ploy. He had already forfeited the $1,000 bail and fled from his home on 209 East 18th Street to Riverside, California, with his wife, Louisa, his daughter, Martina, and half a million dollars in cash. He got his American Dream.

McGurk had made a killing in the real estate market with other properties, some of which were flats on 77th Street. But true to form, even these abodes were described by one magistrate as a "resort for disorderly women and thieves." It was the McGurk element.

Despite all the horrible stuff McGurk witnessed and supported, he was supposedly shocked and heartbroken when his daughter had to pay the price for his misdeeds. She was denied admission to a Catholic convent school in California when it was discovered who her father was. He learned that every dream has a price. McGurk died in California on January 29, 1913, at the age of fifty-nine.

The McGurk legend didn't end there. Suicide Hall rose to national fame after it was described in literary works. The most famous mention was in Mae West's novel, *Diamond Lil*, in which she titled her second chapter, "Suicide Hall."

As for the building, it took on several more incarnations. In the 1950s, it became a skid flophouse called the Liberty Hotel, whose placard outside the front door read, "When did you write to your mother?" In the 1960s, it was an artist co-op and a refuge for women artists. However, the Cooper Square Urban Renewal Project evicted them in 1999.

At one point local citizens put in a petition to save 295 Bowery Street from demolition and requested that the Landmarks Preservation Commission give the building landmark status. It was denied on the basis that it did not have "sufficient historical, cultural or architectural merit." By that time someone had put a big black skull on the outside of the building—a fitting final touch.

In April of 2005, firemen came to the location and took the windows out of the building in preparation for its demolition. The next day they covered the entire building with a drop cloth, as if covering a corpse. Avalon Bay Communities razed the building, which had managed to last 104 years after McGurk was thrown off the premises.

Today, where the old McGurk's Suicide Hall once stood on the Bowery between Houston and East First Streets, stands Avalon Bowery Place, a $300 million, sleek, nondescript huge glass condominium complex, complete with 36,000 square feet of retail space. The building was marketed as "housing for yuppies" with a NoLIta (North of Little Italy) boutique atmosphere. A Whole Foods has moved in, which is a far cry from what the ladies of the evening and the other patrons were being served up while they wallowed in the dark, seedy spaces of the infamous Suicide Hall. The *New York Times* once called the Bowery "the liveliest mile on the face of the earth during 1880–1895." Hopefully, in the annals of history, suicide by jumping from a tall building or drinking carbolic acid is no longer a lively pastime and is one fad that won't be repeated.

CHAPTER 10

The Beautiful Cigar Girl

Twenty-year-old Mary Cecilia Rogers was a beautiful girl with a famous "dark smile" that was said to cast a spell over half the men of New York City. She had worked as a clerk behind the counter of John Anderson's Tobacco Emporium on lower Broadway near Duane Street since she was seventeen. Men came from all over the city to buy cigars from this lovely creature and that is exactly what Anderson counted on; he paid her a generous wage to keep the admirers coming. Many believed Anderson's success was tied to the magnetic powers of young Mary.

Men were infatuated with Mary. One man said he spent an entire afternoon at the cigar store just so he could exchange "teasing glances" with her. Another admirer was inspired to write a poem and had it published in the *New York Herald,* in which he described her "heaven-like smile and her star-like eyes." Others tried a different tack and would boast of their successful business ventures loudly enough so she could hear, in hopes that this would make her think of them as perfect suitors. But Mary played it cool. She would cast her eyes downward and pretend not to hear all the obvious advances. Sometimes she couldn't avoid hearing them and would pretend to be in shock at the coarse language and would daintily hold her hands over her mouth. But Mary knew exactly the power she had and how to keep the men in line.

Because she was so young and so well liked, many worried that ill fate might befall her if she kept hanging around the rough company known to frequent the cigar store.

How did so many know about her? The cigar store was also a popular hangout for writers. Such notables as Washington Irving, James Fenimore Cooper, and Edgar Allan Poe were regulars there. In addition, many newspapermen and editors of the city's largest newspapers and "penny presses" (equivalents of today's tabloids) frequented the place and would often write commentary about her.

The *New York Morning Herald* wrote, "Something should be done instantly to remedy the great evil consequent upon very beautiful girls being placed in cigar and confectionery stores. Designing rich rascals drop into these places, buy cigars and sugar plums, gossip with the girl and ultimately affect her ruin." Yes, everyone loved Mary, who became known as "the beautiful cigar girl," and many wanted to protect her.

But Mary was an independent sort. With the money she earned from the tobacco store, she was able to buy a small boarding house on Nassau Street (aka Publishers' Row) near City Hall, in New York City. She and her frail, sixty-two-year-old widowed mother, Phoebe Rogers, ran the place. Immediately, some of the boarders fell in love with Mary. One was Alfred Crommelin, a rich attorney. Mary's mother approved of this union, but Mary rejected it. Being a gentleman, Crommelin didn't push, but remained a good friend and business advisor to both of them. Like a good girl, Mary would attend church with her mother regularly, and afterwards go off to visit friends. But like many a teenager she also liked her freedom and had a habit of going on unannounced mini vacations.

On October 5, 1838, when she was only seventeen, she decided to go to Brooklyn to visit some relatives for several days. The only problem was she did not tell her mother, friends, or employer where she was going. This caused a huge commotion. The *New York Sun* reported that Miss Mary Cecelia Rogers had disappeared from her home. They claimed that the mother found a suicide note. Anderson's business immediately went downhill. When Mary returned home, she was shocked and angry that everyone was so upset and worried. Some say the "disappearance" was a publicity stunt put together by Anderson, the cigar store owner, to generate interest once he found out about her disappearance. It was later dismissed as a hoax. The truth is she did go away and some believe it was to elope with a secret lover, a dark-complexioned, young naval officer. Apparently this didn't come to fruition.

Mary continued to work at Anderson's place and men continued to fall in love with her. One such man was Daniel Payne, an alcoholic cork cutter who was also a boarder at Mary's place. Naturally Phoebe and Crommelin, her rejected suitor, were not happy with this. Then in June of 1841, Mary announced her engagement to Payne. This caused a month's worth of arguments with her mother, and Mary promised she would not marry him.

Shortly after that, Mary started hinting to Crommelin that she might be interested in him. He ignored her. Finally she just out and out begged for an "emergency" loan. He still did not respond to her. Mary turned to her boss, Anderson, and got the money.

On the Sunday morning of July 25, 1841, Mary was up to her old tricks. She went to church dressed in a white dress, black shawl, blue scarf, Leghorn hat, light-colored shoes, and, to top it all off, a light-colored parasol. Afterward she talked to a friend for a bit. Then she went back to the boarding house and spoke to Payne. She told Payne that she was going to visit a relative of hers, a Mrs. Downing. Since she knew her mother had gotten upset last time, she told Payne that if she did not come home in time for supper to come and "fetch her."

That night, however, New York City was hit with a severe thunderstorm, so when Mary did not come home, instead of worrying, Payne figured Mary used her common sense and stayed the night and would return the next morning. He did not go to fetch her.

When Monday morning came and she had not shown up at home or at work, Anderson, Payne, and Crommelin began to worry. They started a methodical search. They headed over to Mrs. Downing's house, but she said she hadn't seen Mary at all on Sunday, nor had she been expecting her to visit. This got them even more upset. They started going to all the places they thought Mary might have gone. At first her mother seemed calm, probably because Mary had done this before, but as the days passed, her panic mounted.

They placed a notice in the *New York Sun* newspaper asking anyone who had information as to her whereabouts to please come forward and inform her mother at the boarding house, as it is "supposed some accident has befallen her."

A few days later on Wednesday, July 28, on the New Jersey shore, James Boylard and Henry Mallin were spending an afternoon off from work at a popular day trip retreat in Hoboken to get away from the hustle and bustle of New York City. The retreat, known as Sybil's Cave and Spring, was a manmade cave built in 1832 by the Stevens family as a tourist trap in Elysian Fields, a park they made public on their privately owned property. Inside the structure was a natural spring located along the Hudson River, which tourists could access by a Stevens-run ferry from Manhattan. Thousands of people would come and buy the pure water with "beneficial and medicinal properties" for a penny a glass, and then sit at the tables outside. The cave was located between Eighth and Ninth Streets. (Today the cave is buried with overgrowth at the bottom of the hill at the Stevens Institute of Technology on Frank Sinatra Drive.)

As the two friends walked along the lushly wooded River Walk, they happened to gaze out upon the Hudson. In the near distance, they noticed what appeared to be clothing floating in the river. Quickly the men went to a nearby dock, commandeered a rowboat, and rowed out to see what the object was. They were astonished to discover the battered body of a young woman. They tried several times to pull the body over the side of the boat, but could not pull it in. Finally, they had no choice but to lasso the body and tow it back to shore.

A crowd had now gathered. Word spread and the police and newspapers were notified. People stood around in horror at the bruised and beaten body. One of the reporters from the *Herald* described her body: ". . . she was laying on the bank, on her back, with a rope tied around her, and a large stone attached to it . . . her forehead and face appeared to have been battered and butchered, to a mummy. On her head she wore a bonnet, light gloves on her hands, with long watery fingers peering out. . . . Her features were scarcely visible, so much violence had been done on her . . . she presented the most horrible spectacle that the eye could see."

The local Justice of the Peace took information, gathered witnesses' names, and began an investigation. The body was sent to the Hoboken coroner, Richard Cook, to await identification. The coroner did a thorough examination and described the state of the corpse:

> . . . her face was swollen, the veins were highly distended. There was an echymose mark about the size and shape of a man's thumb on the right side of the neck, near the jugular vein, and two or three marks on the left side resembling the shape of a man's fingers, which led me to believe she had been throttled and partially choked by a man's hand. It appeared as if the wrists had been tied together, and as if she had raised her hands to try to tear something from off her mouth and neck, which was choking and strangling her. The dress was much torn in several places . . . a piece was torn clean out of this garment, about a foot or 18 inches in width . . . this same piece was tied round her mouth, with a hard knot at the back part of the neck; I think this was done to smother her cries and that it was probably held tight round her mouth by one of her brutal ravishers. Her hat was off her head at the time of the outrage, and that after her violation and murder had been completed, it was tied on. . . .

The doctor concluded that "positively the poor girl had been brutally violated" while being held down on her back and not on a

Twenty-year-old Mary Rogers was known as the beautiful cigar girl, and
had many admirers who would come to Anderson's Tobacco Emporium in
Manhattan just to be able to look at her. She was brutally murdered in 1841,
and the case is still unsolved.
DRAWING COURTESY OF JAN TURNER OF CARSON WORLDWIDE

bed, but on some kind of board. He went on to say, but "there was
not the slightest trace of pregnancy" and so therefore the woman
"had evidently been a person of chastity and correct habits" and
that the murder was done by "more than two or three persons."

The newspapers rolled out the story. Although finding dead
bodies floating in the water around New York due to gang violence

was unfortunately not an uncommon occurrence in the mid-1800s, one person coming forth changed the whole dynamic. Alfred Crommelin came forward and identified the body—it was Mary Rogers. It was a hard sight for the police and Crommelin to see her so disfigured, to see beauty transformed by brutality. Crommelin broke down and cried. He also brought back a lock of Mary's hair and pieces of her clothing to her bereaved mother.

Word got out that the "Beautiful Cigar Girl" had been murdered. Curiosity seekers now flooded the area of Sybil's Cave. The tabloids speculated on the clues and suspects of the "Mary Rogers

Sybil's Cave is the oldest manmade structure in Hoboken, created in 1832 by the Stevens family as a folly on their property that contained a natural spring, where they would charge people a penny a glass to drink the water. It was near this cave that the beautiful cigar girl's body was found. It is located between 8th and 9th Streets at the foot of Stevens Institute of Technology on Frank Sinatra Drive, in Hoboken, New Jersey. The cave is gated up, but there is talk on and off about its reopening to the public.

Tragedy," with the first finger of accusation pointed at her fiancé, Daniel Payne. Payne quickly produced sworn affidavits from witnesses to his whereabouts before, during, and after Mary's mysterious disappearance. The affidavits convinced the papers, and both the *New York Times* and the *Evening Star* made it clear that, in their eyes, Payne was "exonerated from even a shadow of suspicion."

As police investigations continued, so did speculation in the penny tabloids. James Gordon Bennett, editor of the *New York Herald,* wrote that Mary was done in by one of the brutal gangs of the times. He went on to form a citizens committee and berated the police and government officials for not finding the killers. He offered a reward for information leading to the murderers and their arrest.

It's important to note that at the time New York City only had a population of 320,000 and there really was no "police force." There was a day force called "roundmen," a night watch called "leatherheads," and six justices of the police who were all corrupt and bought by local politicians. The total force sent to solve the Mary Rogers's case consisted of one night watch, one hundred city marshals, thirty-one constables, and fifty-one "police officers."

The media seized the story and used it to see which one could sell the most papers. For the first time in history, tabloid reporters went out to do "investigative reporting." Their findings bordered on fiction disguised as truth until proven otherwise. The *New York Evening Post* named a gang member, James Finnegan, suspect and said that he had been seen wearing "a ring which is said to have been . . . one belonging to Mary Rogers." Nothing came of this claim, and some believe the paper invented it to sell more papers.

Another paper, the *Evening Tattler,* claimed that Mary was not dead. It theorized that Crommelin could not possibly have identified Mary in that decomposed state. The paper went on to say that, scientifically, a body thrown into the Hudson on a Sunday could not have risen by Wednesday because it would take six to ten days for it to decompose and float back up. As a result of the article, Payne was asked to identify the body a second time. New York governor William H. Seward even got involved, hoping to get leads by announcing in several newspapers a $750 reward for any information that would help the police solve the crime.

The police investigated a constant parade of suspects: Arthur Crommelin and Daniel Payne, both of whom had solid alibis; William Kiekuck, a young sailor who had once boarded at the Rogers place; Joseph Moore, a wood engraver who worked down the block; and John Anderson, Mary's employer. None of them could be charged with the crime. With no new suspects, interest in the case was dying down, until a "new" discovery came to light.

A month had now passed and Mrs. Frederica Loss, who owned a tavern called Nick Moore's House in the Weehawken and Hoboken area (between Sybil's Cave and Elysian Fields), came forward and said that two of her three sons had discovered women's clothing and a woman's monogrammed handkerchief with the initials M. R. in a nearby thicket. She said that the clothes had been discovered on August 25, but she had waited a few days before calling the police. Upon inspection, the rumpled clothes were mildewed as if they had been lying there for weeks. That area became dubbed "the Murder Thicket."

This renewed interest in the story did not bring in any new leads. One thing that it did bring in, though, was more business to Loss's tavern, and as more people came in, Loss's celebrity status grew and, remarkably, she seemed to have more "recollections" to tell reporters.

Loss suddenly "remembered" that Mary Rogers had come in on Sunday, July 25, to her tavern around 4 p.m., accompanied by man with a dark complexion. They drank and then left arm in arm. Later that evening, Loss claimed she had heard a scream nearby and thought it was one of her sons who had gotten hurt. She ran outside, saw her children were okay, and then forgot about the scream.

While the *Herald News* found this to be "evidence" that Mary was murdered by a gang, the *Evening Tattler* felt that the tavern owner was spinning a tale. They found it hard to believe that Mary's clothes had suddenly appeared in the thicket a month later. In the pile of "newfound clothes" was a pair of women's gloves, which was odd because the corpse of Mary Rogers had gloves on when it was found. The *Evening Tattler* concluded that someone who did not know all the details of the case planted the clothing there. Hudson historian Raymond Paul later confirmed this theory as true.

During this time, her loved ones were devastated, especially Mary's fiancé, Payne, who moved out of the boarding house shortly after Mary's murder. Already an alcoholic, the cork cutter went into a deep depression. He claimed Mary's ghostly apparitions appeared to him on a regular basis. Payne was on the brink of insanity.

On October 7, 1841, he started the day by getting as drunk as he could. Then he stopped by a store and purchased a bottle of the poison laudanum, aka tincture of opium, which is considered a potent narcotic and was used to treat a variety of ailments back then, mainly coughs. (Today this is a highly regulated and controlled substance throughout the world, but back then it was easily available.)

He rode the ferry to Hoboken, stopped by Loss's tavern, and asked for directions to the thicket where Mary's clothes had been found. He went to the thicket, sat down, and wrote a note: "To the World here I am on the very spot. May God forgive me for my misspent life." Then he downed the poison. Eventually, after another bout of drinking, he lay down on the spot and died. The papers viewed him not as a suspect but as a heartbroken lover who could no longer exist without his beloved.

The story just would not die, yet it could not be solved. Edgar Allan Poe, the then-unemployed, opium-addicted mystery writer, was also following it closely. He, too, had been smitten with Mary. The case of Mary's mysterious disappearance sparked an idea for a short story, with Mary as the main character. Poe had his own ending in mind.

Meanwhile, in October of 1842, the tavern lady, Frederica Loss, was accidentally shot by one of her own sons. For two weeks she lay dying, and near the end, she called the newspapers in for one last revelation. She had been in and out of consciousness and said Mary's ghost had been haunting her, so she felt the need to tell the truth.

Loss said that on the afternoon of Mary's murder, Mary came into her tavern to drink but it was for a reason. It was known by some that Mrs. Loss was associated with a Madam Restell, aka the

"Madam Killer." Restell had a home in Greenwich Street for unwed mothers. Her philosophy was that the only "plausible birth control system was abortion."

At the time, the law and a large number of rich clients supported her private practice. But for poorer people, she franchised out her abortion work to people like Mrs. Loss. The dark-complexioned man who was with Mary could have been the abortionist. (That point was never made clear by Mrs. Loss.) Mrs. Loss said Mary had an abortion near her inn and that she died from complications. This would explain the need for the "emergency loan" and possibly the scream heard from the direction of the thicket.

According to the newspapers, her body was "taken at night by Loss's sons and sunk in the river where it was later found. Mary's clothes were first sunk in a pond on the land of (a neighbor); but it was afterwards thought that they were not safe there, and they were accordingly taken and scattered through the woods as they were found."

Investigations again ensued, this time centering on several bloody spots in the thicket and those found on Mary's clothes, which, it was speculated, could have come from an abortion. It was also speculated that her bonds were used to keep her from screaming during the abortion. The story still didn't explain the beating, but it might, some argued, shed new light on wounds that were previously thought to be from a gang rape.

Many others did not believe this deathbed confession because it contradicted the coroner's original findings. The coroner's report had shown that beyond doubt Mary was a "person of chastity and correct habits" and had been murdered. (Some believe however, the abortion doctor paid money to the coroner to keep Mary's reputation spotless because she was so well loved.) Either way, many still discredited Loss's testimony because she was drifting in and out of consciousness, babbling in broken English and German while she was revealing details of the "true" incident.

Shortly after their mother's death, the two eldest Loss sons, who supposedly stumbled upon Mary's clothes in the murder thicket, were charged with the illegal disposal of a body. But because of the lack of evidence and witnesses, and their mom's babbling "confession," the charges were dropped and they were released.

By then (1842) Edgar Allan Poe had published his story "The Mystery of Marie Roget." Poe's story was set in Paris (instead of New York), and his detective, C. Auguste Dupin, and his sidekick, the unnamed narrator, showed conclusively that the character Marie had been murdered by a young naval officer of dark complexion who had previously attempted to elope with her. He dragged her body to the water and deposited it there after a botched abortion attempt that he called a "premature delivery." Poe's story, with its echoes of Mary's real life, worked its way into the general consciousness and became the accepted explanation of Mary Rogers's murder for 150 years. Poe was so convinced he had truly solved the crime with his deductive reasoning that in the story's introduction he boldly wrote, "All argument founded upon the fiction is applicable to the truth: and the investigation of the truth was the object."

Mary's death and the constant criticism aimed at the "police force" helped create the Police Reform Act of 1845. It was also significant in creating an 1845 law criminalizing abortion in New York. (In 1970, New York repealed its 1845 law and allowed abortions up to the twenty-fourth week.) Poe died shortly after in 1849 while the case was still unsolved.

In 1887, the case resurfaced when another strange suspicion came to light. The *New York Times* was covering the legal battle over John Anderson's fortune (he was Mary's employer at the tobacco store). The *Times* quoted one counsel's suggestion that "John Anderson gave Poe $5000 to write the story of Marie Roget, in order to draw people's attention away from himself, who many believed, was her murderer." It was never proven whether Poe accepted Anderson's offer or if it was even ever made to him, but Poe was a struggling author so it's possible. Either way, the *Times'* reporting once again cast suspicion and opened the case.

Eventually, Sybil's Cave was cemented shut to keep curiosity seekers away. It was briefly reopened in 2008 with plans to make it a tourist attraction, but those plans died in 2011, and it has since been taken over by nature and a locked gate.

Every effort has been made by police, investigators, the media, and criminologists past and present to solve the case, but in the end it was and still is an unsolved murder case with no indictments, no trial, and no formal resolution.

The question still remains: Who killed Mary Rogers? Was it one of the notorious urban gangs? Was it a lone assassin known to her or not? Was it Poe himself who talked incessantly about Mary's murder with Anderson? Was it Anderson trying to get more publicity for his shop? Was it murder by the naval lover whom she disappeared with the first time? Did he find out she was pregnant and kill her after the abortion? And who was the dark-complexioned man, a lover or a doctor? Did the botched abortion really kill her? And if Mary did have an abortion, whose baby was it? Some say it could have been Crommelin's and that's why Mary went to him for the money. Others say Mary was offered up as a prostitute at the boarding house, resulting in the need for the botched and fatal abortion.

Still others like author Raymond Paul believe it was the despondent Daniel Payne who murdered her not on that Sunday (when he had an airtight alibi), but on the following Tuesday, when it was known Payne was in the area. He theorizes that Payne knew she was having the abortion and was going to pick her up, but jealousy made him kill her. Paul also conjectures that because rigor mortis sets in within twenty-four hours of death, and the Hudson waters in July would not have been cold enough to slow down the process, the stiffness of the body proves that she could not have been killed any earlier than Tuesday after she recovered from the abortion. Later Payne could not take what he had done and committed suicide.

Whatever the truth, the tragedy, the murder, and the mystery of Mary Rogers, the beautiful cigar girl, are still compelling. Mary's story remains one of the most puzzling unsolved cases of murder on the record books of New York City.

CHAPTER 11

The Friendly Ghost Hostess of Skene Manor

Whitehall is a town at the northeast quadrant of New York. In 1759 a British Army colonel named Philip Skene built sawmills, gristmills, and an iron foundry in the town. He later founded the town, and originally named it after himself, Skenesborough.

When the Revolutionary War rolled around, one of Skene's trading schooners was captured. This caused Benedict Arnold, the American Revolutionary general and traitor, to build a fleet of ships in Whitehall. The Whitehall harbor also built ships for the US Navy that were used during the War of 1812, and so in 1960, the New York State Legislature declared Whitehall the legendary birthplace of the US Navy.

Because of Skene's service to the British Crown, and since at that time they were still winning the war, King George III rewarded him with a large plot of land on which to build a modest home for himself and his wife, Katherine. Katherine came from a very wealthy family, and although she loved Philip, she wanted to make sure that her money would not be squandered if she happened to die first. Skene had promised his beloved that one day he would build her a castle. Katherine wanted to make sure this castle would come to fruition, so she added a clause to her will that stated an annuity would be paid to the colonel only "as long as my body lies above ground." She of course meant as long as she was alive.

Unfortunately for her, she died before the colonel. The good colonel wanted to honor his wife's final wishes, so he shrewdly buried her "above ground," thus keeping the provisions of her will intact and the monies rolling in so he could continue to live off her wealth. He was said to have honored his beloved by embalming her in vinegar and placing her in a lead coffin that he kept propped up in a basement corner. He lived that way quite nicely for a while.

However, in 1777 when the Americans started to win the war, Skene skedaddled to Canada and, of course, took the cash with him. He left his home, promising to pick up his wife's remains. Of course, he never did.

Katherine was not happy propped up there in the corner. But what happened next made her even unhappier. When Benedict Arnold and his invading troops took over Skene's land, they discovered Katherine's lead casket. They had no problem taking the woman out of her casket, stealing her jewelry, and then melting the casket down and turning it into lead musket balls. Her body was buried unceremoniously on the mountain somewhere. She was not a happy dead person.

So she did what any self-respecting ghost would do, she started to haunt the soldiers that were guarding the grounds. She would mysteriously appear before them at night and then dissolve into a ball of shimmering light. Needless to say, this scared the soldiers so much that they requested to be removed from night watch duty.

Some versions of the story have it that Skene buried his wife honorably on the mountain and did not prop her up in the basement. In this version, the soldiers found her buried in her lead casket, used the casket for musket balls, and she haunted them for that. No one is sure of the true story.

Either way, the land was eventually bought by Melancton Wheeler, but nothing was done to it. For nearly a hundred years, the land remained as it was. Then in 1867 the New York State Supreme Court Judge Joseph H. Potter bought the land from Wheeler and decided to spruce up the place. His first order of business was to tear down the old house. In 1874, he hired artisans from Italy, and using native gray sandstone from the rock of Skene Mountain and wood from the surrounding area, he built a massive Victorian Gothic stone mansion in its place. The building was all hand-carved and handcrafted. It cost him approximately $25,000 to build. The roof was made of slate, there were five chimneys, and gorgeous wrought-iron ridges on the roof. It had six dormers and decorative pediments in the peak of the main tower.

There were beautifully carved wood brackets around the building. Inside the building were eight fireplaces, one of marble and slate. (One was later removed when they refurbished the kitchen.) The banisters on the staircase were made of the finest mahogany, walnut, oak, and birch woods, and multicolored stained glass windows hung over the front entrance and at the top of the stairs. The walls were papered with detailed hunting scenes, and the ceilings had dark wooden beams.

All this beauty and grandeur caught Katherine's attention. She heard a commotion and felt that at long last she was getting her castle. Being the woman of the house, she felt the need to take an active part in overseeing the construction and would be seen by workers who were building the place. She was delighted when the place was filled with the most lavish furniture. Potter named his home "Mountain Terrace." After the judge's death in 1906, his widow, who was also named Catherine, sold the manor to Edgar Lowenstein, who added a carriage house, installed gas fixtures, and put in a heating system. Now the mansion was called "Lowen's Castle." However, it didn't matter what the mansion was called, Katherine Skene roamed the place overseeing the changes that were being made to "her" home.

Skene Manor changed hands many times; new owners added their own touches. In 1922 the owner of the house was Dr. Theodore Sachs, a jeweler, clock expert, and optometrist. He added the clock to the manor tower as his contribution. Once again a war laid claim to the mansion, this time in 1942, when the lead from the clock was used to make bullets.

In 1946 the manor changed hands yet again. This time the owners, Clayton and Pauline Shear, were entrepreneurs. They bought the mansion to use as a business. They renamed it "Skene Manor" in honor of the village founder. It became a combination restaurant, bed-and-breakfast, and dinner theater. To heighten the interest for their patrons, they highlighted the history of the place, complete with the story of Katherine's casket being stuck in the corner by her husband. To add some realism to the story, they put a coffin in the bar and rigged a floating hand behind a curtain that would move via string for unsuspecting and often drunk customers. This of course left many running from the bar, claiming to have seen Katherine's decrepit floating hand pointing to some unknown mystery, further enhancing the many ghost stories surrounding the manor.

But long after the parlor tricks subsided, many still claimed to see the hand floating above the water fountain, supposedly wearing a large "bauble on one finger." Maybe this was one of Katherine's favorite pieces of jewelry that the invading troops had not gotten their hands on when they robbed her grave.

The manor continued to change hands, and they were not all Katherine's. The Reynolds owned it from 1951 to 1968 and then sold it to Leo and Florence Mulholland, who owned it from 1968 to 1983. While under their ownership, in May of 1974, the manor was put on the National Register of Historic Places and, of course, the ghostly stories continued.

In 1980 one of the Mulholland's boarders related a ghostly tale. He claimed that one night he was awakened out of a deep sleep by a very loud sound. During his investigation, he put his ear to the door and heard "creepy sounds of someone moving about in the hallway." Frightened, he decided to barricade himself in the bedroom by placing his own bed against the door. He figured that if anyone tried to come into his bedroom he would be immediately awakened and he could defend himself against the intruder. He soon managed to quiet his fears and fell back into a deep sleep. The next morning when he got up, he was shocked to discover that both he and the bed had been pushed away from the door. He was never able to sleep comfortably in that house again.

Another resident, Tim Shenk, a training sergeant in the town's National Guard unit in Whitehall, used to play the guitar in the restaurant and bar. He said the place was definitely haunted back then and that he had some "pretty freaky stuff happen every now and then."

Exterior of Skene Manor, said to be haunted by Katherine Skene. Legend has it that she was buried aboveground and kept in a lead coffin by her military husband during the Revolutionary War. The manor is opened for tours and is located on top of the hill at 8 Potter Terrace in Whitehall, New York.

With tales like these, the building kept being bought and sold. In between owners, the building would remain vacant and when the new owner would move in, he or she would once again try to renovate it.

Another Katherine tale has it that a day laborer was doing construction work in the basement of the manor when he heard a loud rapping on the front door. Annoyed at being disturbed at his work, he decided to ignore it. But the person at the door was relentless. So he went upstairs and opened the door. Standing in front of him was a very worried looking female traveler.

She asked him, "Oh, sir, are you alright?"

The man replied, "Yes, of course I'm alright. Why do you ask?"

She explained, "Well, I was driving along the road and I happened to look up and I saw this woman waving frantically from the second-floor window, motioning for me to come and help. I couldn't resist, I had places to go, but I had to see if she was okay."

The worker laughed and said, "Well as you can see I'm fine, there is nothing going on. I was working on renovations in the basement. This house is unoccupied. No one is here but me."

He had no sooner gotten the words out of his mouth than both of them heard a tremendous noise from the basement. They ran downstairs, and in exactly the spot where the man had been working before he answered the door, stood a mass of rubble. Everything had collapsed: the bricks, the wood, the plaster, some stone; whatever was in that area had come down. Had the worker not moved from that spot just moments earlier to answer the door, he would have died or have been seriously injured. Many believe it was Katherine (or some other spirit) that signaled the woman traveler to distract the worker and thus save his life.

In 1995, an offer was made to dismantle the building and move it out of state. Concerned citizens formed Whitehall, Skene Manor Preservation Inc., aka S.O.S. (Save Our Skene). They raised funds and on October 26, 1995, they purchased the place. It was placed on the National Register of Historic Places. According to their president, Joanne Ingalls, when they took over the place, it was "literally falling apart. The previous owner pilfered everything of value from the building, from the chandeliers right down to the doorknobs." Today it offers free tours, a tearoom for lunch, and a gift shop.

As for ghosts, some say the place is ghost free; others feel Katherine's spirit still remains. According to Joanne, one of the docents at Skene Manor, "Katherine Skene is here and she loves us and takes care of us. No matter how many people see her, we all adore her. Every morning we say, 'Good Morning, Katherine,' and when we leave at night we say, 'Goodbye, Katherine.'"

Whether the ghost of Katherine still remains is for each visitor to decide. One thing is for sure, after all these years, she finally got her castle. Now that is one persistent woman ghost.

CHAPTER 12

The Unlucky General Slocum

The September 11, 2001, terrorist attacks were the worst disaster in terms of loss of life in a single day in New York history. Before that, however, there was the tragedy of the *General Slocum*.

The PS *General Slocum* was a triple-decker, two-sided wheel, steam passenger ship built by the Devine Burtis shipbuilding company in Brooklyn, New York, in 1891. It was 264 feet long and weighed 1,281 tons. Each side wheel of the *Slocum* had twenty-six rotating paddles thirty-one feet in diameter. It could reach a maximum speed of sixteen knots, making it the fastest boat in New York at the time. The *Slocum* had three decks, three engines, and three watertight compartments.

The decks were adorned with fine artwork and furniture, and the food was said to be excellent. The ship could comfortably accommodate three thousand passengers and was one of the most popular steamships of its day. It would transport passengers every weekend and holidays from May to October, bringing them from Manhattan to nearby resort locations like the Rockaways, Sandy Hook, and parts of Long Island. For those who didn't like crowds, private groups could rent the boat for a day's excursion. It took about twenty-two men to crew the ship, and it was usually captained by William H. Van Schaick with the aid of two additional copilots.

Unfortunately, almost from its start, this ship adorned with beauty was cursed with bad luck. It was either that or the captain just didn't know how to steer the darn thing.

Just four months after its launch, the *Slocum* ran aground in Rockaway, New York, and tugboats had to come to its rescue. Three years later, on July 29, 1894, the ship hit a sandbar so hard that the electrical generator went out. There were 4,700 passengers crammed on board that day, way over the capacity limit. They were not very happy, but luckily no one got hurt during the incident.

A month later, in August, a storm caused the *Slocum* to hit dirt right off of Coney Island. This time the passengers had to be transferred to another boat. The following month the *Slocum* ran smack into the tugboat, the *R. T. Sayre,* in the East River. The collision caused a lot of damage to the steering, although with the ship's track record, it might seem as if the steering had already been faulty.

Four years later, in July of 1898, the *General Slocum* collided with another ship called the *Amelia.* Three years after that on August 17, 1901, a different kind of encounter took place. The *Slocum* was carrying nine hundred drunken anarchists. Being under the influence, these passengers got a little rowdy and started a riot. Like a band of pirates, they tried to take control of the ship. The twenty-two crew members fought back and managed to keep control, which was not bad considering the odds. The captain docked the ship at the police pier and seventeen of the drunken rioters were arrested.

In June 1902, with four hundred passengers on board for a delightful day of excursions around New York City, the ship once again ran aground. This time a tug couldn't get it out so fast and the passengers had to camp out for the night.

But the worst was yet to come. On Wednesday, June 15, 1904, Reverend George Hass decided to charter the popular paddleboat for $350. The reverend ran the St. Mark's Evangelical Lutheran Church located on East Sixth Street between Second and Third Avenues in the heart of Kleindeutschland, more commonly known as the Little Germany district of Manhattan. Little Germany ran from the East River at Houston Street to 14th Street—today the area is known as the East Village. At the time one-third of the population of New York was German. (As a side note, when New Yorkers think about a historical German neighborhood, they think of Yorkville or "German Broadway," which was centered around 86th Street, and extended from 83rd to 93rd Streets from Lexington Avenue and the East End until the 1960s. The Germans' move uptown was a result of the disaster that was soon to unfold.)

Hass wanted to take his congregation of working-class German immigrants on a picnic to celebrate the end of the Sunday school year. They had been holding this annual picnic for seventeen consecutive years.

Since the day of the excursion was a workday, most of the 1,300 plus passengers on the *General Slocum* were women and children; half of the people were under twenty years old. The exact number of passengers has never been confirmed.

The day's itinerary was to sail up the East River, then head east toward Long Island Sound to Locust Grove, their chosen picnic area, for a day of food, games, and fun. There were thirty-five crewmen on board to take care of the passengers.

The young parishioners boarded the *General Slocum* from the East Third Street pier near Houston Street at nine o'clock. A band was in full swing, greeting them with popular German music. At 9:40 a.m. the recently overhauled ship departed with people cheering and flags waving. Everyone was excited. Children were laughing and playing, and hundreds of them were jammed into the upper deck to wave to people and take in the sights. Mothers were watching their broods and chatting with the other church ladies. Everything was sailing smoothly—for the first half hour.

Then tragedy struck. At 10 a.m. as the ship was passing East 90th Street near Randall's Island, a twelve-year-old boy noticed some smoke. He ran to warn the captain but was shooed away.

A spark, probably from a carelessly tossed crewman's match, ignited a barrel of straw below the main deck in a small lamp room in the forward section of the ship. The room was filled with flammable liquids, paints, and gasoline. Several crewmen tried to put out the fire, but they had never had any emergency safety training and weren't quite sure what to do first. They ran to get the fire hoses, but the hoses were rotted out and actually burst and disintegrated when the crew turned on the water and tried to use them. They notified the captain that there was a fire on board. A full ten minutes had gone by, and in that short time, the fire was already raging out of control.

Learning that the ship was on fire, the captain had to make a quick decision. After all, his vessel was only a few hundred feet from shore when the fire broke out. He could run the ship aground or stop at a nearby landing so passengers could get away from the floating inferno.

He decided he would do that, but he later claimed that a nearby tugboat captain who feared that flames from the ship would ignite oil tanks and the riverside buildings yelled for him not to stop. With no other choice, the captain decided to go full steam ahead to North Brother Island, which was only minutes away. But his decision proved deadly because as he headed into the winds, the speed fanned the fire and spread it more quickly due to the highly flammable paint that coated the wooden ship.

Onlookers watched in horror and yelled to the captain to dock the ship. Others jumped into boats and followed the inferno so they could rescue any passengers who might go overboard.

Panicked shouts of "Fire!" echoed through the ship. Mothers went screaming for their children. No one was sure where to run for safety. Since the crew had never conducted a fire drill either for themselves or the passengers, and the safety equipment had never been maintained, the passengers and crew were on their own.

The three thousand life jackets on board were worthless. They had been manufactured in 1891 by the Nonpareil Cork Works Company. In order to cut costs, the company had filled them with cheap granulate cork, and to bring the jackets up to their proper weight, had used iron bars inside. In addition, these jackets were covered with canvas that had rotted over time, and the cork inside had turned to dust. They were also nailed tight to the overhead by rusty wiring. But why did no one know that? Because these jackets had never been used! They had hung above the deck, unusable and rotting for thirteen years.

When desperate mothers ripped down the jackets to try to save the lives of their children, they had no idea what they were doing. They put the rotted life jackets on their children and threw them overboard to protect them from burning to death.

They watched in horror as their children, instead of floating to safety, sank to their deaths. Screams of despair were heard throughout the ship.

The six lifeboats were just as useless. They were tied up and could not be moved because they had recently been painted and the dried paint glued them to their chocks, rendering all of the boats inaccessible. And even if they could manage to pry them off and get them into the water, they would have capsized because the captain was driving like a madman to get to the island.

It was massive frenzy as people trampled over each other. One woman, while looking for her son and mother, spotted three babies that were being stomped to death. She managed to scoop them up, but as she did so, she spotted her son. She ran toward him but got crushed, lost hold of the babies, and lost sight of her son as well. That was the last she ever saw of him.

The flames were forcing people to huddle en masse, but as they did, the weight made them plummet through the ship's floorboards, which were weakened from the flames. When it seemed like the only choice left was to burn or swim, hundreds hung over the rails and clung on as long as they could before letting go and falling into the water. The turning paddles of the boat mauled them as it forged full steam ahead.

Others who managed to escape the beating of the paddles simply drowned. In those days, swimming was not a popular sport. Americans simply did not know how to swim, so jumping overboard was as unimaginable to them as trying to brave the blazing fire. When they jumped overboard, their heavy wool clothes weighed them down, quickly pulling them to their watery graves.

A few lucky survivors were plucked from the waters by the boats that followed the ship. One little boy who was thrown into the river by his mother clutching his lucky stuffed toy dog managed to survive.

A heroic captain ran his tug alongside the *General Slocum* in full exposure to the fire and saved over a hundred lives. Everyone was trying his or her best to save those who could be saved. For the most part, rescue boats picked up lifeless bodies of women and children that were either burned or drowned. It was horrendous to see so many dead babies and children in the water.

Finally, while the ship was still burning, the captain managed to run it close to shore on North Brother Island, an island that housed people with infectious diseases (and later the infamous Typhoid Mary). They were in about twenty-five feet of swiftly churning water. Seeing this, the hospital staff and some patients rushed to help. They formed a human chain to try to pull victims who jumped out of the water. Others caught children whom parents were tossing overboard. Still others grabbed ladders that were being used to renovate the hospital and put them up against the ship to get people safely on shore.

Within minutes, all who could be saved were pulled from the burning hulk. Some reports say the captain stayed on the ship while his cap was on fire; others say as soon as the ship hit North Brother Island, Van Schaick jumped on a nearby tugboat and deserted his ship. Some reports say he had barely a wound on him, others say he was seriously injured and lost sight in one eye due to the fire. Either way he was hospitalized in Lebanon Hospital and only two of the thirty-five crewmen died.

The current eventually carried the burning inferno a thousand yards until it struck land at Hunts Point in the Bronx. The ship burned to the waterline. Later, divers searched for bodies in the bowels of the ship. Rescue teams combed the area and riverbanks for missing bodies.

Word spread quickly and the newspapers arrived at the scene. Rescue workers were dispatched, and many cried openly at the hundreds of stacked bodies of innocent children. Thousands of family members gathered at the church to await word as to whether their loved ones were alive or not. The East 23rd Street pier was designated as a temporary morgue, and policemen and the coroners laid out hundreds of corpses as they came in. Rescue workers were dispatched to get ice from as many places as they could to preserve the bodies. Others had to locate coffins. As the bodies piled up, the newspapers reported the counts: 500, 600, 700, 800 people dead and counting.

Over the next few days, blackened, charred bodies washed up by the hundreds. Other corpses were brought in by the boatloads. On June 14, 1904, the *New York Times* reported that "grief-crazed crowds" came to identify bodies in open coffins that were lined up by the hundreds. Police had to prevent dozens from throwing themselves in the river due to their sorrow. Funerals were being held every hour on the hour for days in churches all over Little Germany.

Headlines about the *General Slocum* disaster went around the world. Money poured in from private citizens and charitable groups from Rhode Island to California. World leaders and European royalty sent money and letters of condolence to the church to help the families. Both stories of heroism and stories of souvenir hunters

On June 15, 1904, brave citizens in row boats mill around in a rescue effort as the steam paddleboat the *General Slocum* sinks in the East River, not far from North Brother Island. In fifteen minutes, an estimated 1,021 passengers and two crew lost their lives.
PHOTO COURTESY OF MICHAEL W. POCOCK AND WWW.MARITIMEQUEST.COM

who would fish the bodies out of the river for their jewelry made the papers for weeks. One particular story in the *New York Times* that angered people was about a private captain who watched the whole tragedy unfold without lifting a finger or launching a boat to help rescue the women and children.

Although to this day there is no definitive death toll, the most common number cited is 1,021 dead, eight hundred of whom were children. This disaster wiped out whole families; in one case, fourteen family members were on board and twelve died.

Immediately after the tragedy, investigations were launched. Many fingers were pointed, and as a result seven people were indicted by a Federal Grand Jury: the captain; the two inspectors who put their stamp of approval on the unsafe life preservers; and the president, secretary, treasurer, and commodore of the

Knickerbocker Steamship Company, which owned the *General Slocum*. Also brought up on charges were the managers of the Non-pareil Cork Works Company that filled the ineffective life jackets.

All escaped conviction except one man, the fall guy, the sixty-eight-year-old captain of the ship, Van Schaick. Since he was the captain, it was felt that he should have been aware of the safety of the ship, top to bottom. Three charges were filed against him: criminal negligence by failing to maintain proper fire drills and fire extinguishers and two charges of manslaughter. He was found guilty on the criminal negligence charge and sentenced up river to ten years hard labor in Sing Sing in Ossining, New York, on February 27, 1908. A parole board under President William Taft released him on December 19, 1912, with a pardon becoming effective on Christmas Day that restored him to full citizenship. He spent a total of three years and six months in prison.

The Steamship Company got off with a slap on the hand; they had to pay a minimal fine, even though it was proven they had bribed two US Steamboat Inspection Service inspectors to say the *Slocum* was safe and sound a month before the disaster.

The neighborhood of Little Germany was never the same again. After the disaster, most of the residents could not handle the trauma of losing their entire families; some moved away, some committed suicide, others went insane.

The tragedy of the *Slocum,* unlike that of the *Titanic* in 1912, was compounded by the fact that everyone on the ship was related in some way, "by blood, marriage, religion, and location." The *Slocum* destroyed not only the passengers' lives, but wiped out an entire community as well.

The red brick Lutheran church building was later bought and became a synagogue.

Victims were buried in cemeteries around New York. Sixty-one unidentified bodies plus several that were recovered many days after the disaster were buried in a common grave.

The last survivor of the *General Slocum* was Adella Wotherspon. She was six months old when the disaster struck. She died on January 26, 2004, at the age of 100.

The ship itself remained on the spot it had drifted to for several weeks. The burnt hulk was later sold for $1,800. It was converted into a barge and renamed the *Maryland,* but even that reincarnation carried bad karma with it—it sprung a leak and sank during a storm in 1911. All three men aboard were saved.

As a result of the tragedy, there was a complete shakedown of government inspectors, and safety laws were put into place. Ships were now required to have fireproof metal bulkheads, working life jackets for each passenger on board, sprinkler systems, fire hoses capable of handling 100 pounds of pressure per square inch, accessible life boats, and mandatory fire drills. One of the only physical remembrances left of the disaster is a nine-foot Tennessee marble memorial of two children looking out to sea in Tompkins Square Park on East Ninth Street and Avenue A in Manhattan. The inscription says, THEY WERE EARTH'S PUREST, CHILDREN YOUNG AND FAIR. It is in the heart of what once was Little Germany. There is also a plaque attached to the iron gate of a synagogue that describes the disaster.

Why was this tragedy forgotten by so many? A number of people cite the 1911 Triangle Shirtwaist Factory fire as the second largest tragedy to hit New York City before 9/11. That only claimed the lives of 146 unfortunate young immigrant women, however. Some believe that anti-German sentiment from World Wars I and II made the *Slocum* take a back seat in New York history. Still others believe that, even though it did not happen on New York soil, the tragedy of the *Titanic* (which took 1,517 lives) outshone the *Slocum* disaster. Even so, the *Slocum* has been described as the "most deadly peacetime maritime disaster in American history."

And there are still many unanswered questions. How could a disaster of this magnitude happen only a hundred feet from the shore of one of the most modern cities in the world? Was it just poor judgment on the part of the captain? Why was the crew so poorly trained? Was it pure greed with no regard for passenger safety? Why did the ship run aground so much? Was it bad judgment in steering or were the waters dangerous? If so, why didn't other ships keep running ashore? How was it that the captain and crew survived when so many others died? What did they do that the passengers didn't?

Why was only the captain indicted when so many others were guilty as well? Was it the corrupt politics of the times—all that was needed was just one scapegoat? And then there is the ultimate question, what really happened? Who started the fire? The cause of the fire remains unknown to this day.

CHAPTER 13

Execution Rocks

When you think of secluded getaways you probably conjure images of bright sunny days, happiness, and romance. But what if the place you are spending the night is a deserted tiny island with a history of torture, fires, shipwrecks, skeletons, ghosts, and as a dumping ground for a serial killer's victims? It would take a brave soul to want to spend a night there, but that is exactly what a night at Execution Rocks offers since it became a national historic landmark.

Execution Rocks (originally known as Executioner's Rock on old sailing charts) is located twenty miles east of Manhattan, a mile offshore at the western end of Long Island Sound, right out of Manhasset Bay, in Port Washington. It's on the border between New Rochelle and Sands Point. For those with a nautical nature it is latitude 40.87800 N and longitude: −73.73.73800 W. There are many dark myths and mysteries surrounding this island and how it got its name.

The first legend, according to the book *The Power Broker*, was that "original slave owning settlers of Sands Point had disposed of 'troublesome slaves' by chaining them to the rock at low tide" and let them drown at the nearby Execution Rocks as punishment for their wrongdoings.

What kind of wrongdoings? Those were not disclosed, but the closest thing one can find to any claim to that story is that in 1741 Manhattan had the second largest slave population of any city in the British-owned thirteen colonies. (The first was Charleston, South Carolina.) Amid whispers of a conspiracy that was about to occur due to tensions between poor whites and slaves over competition for jobs, a series of thirteen fires were set in Lower Manhattan, with the most prominent being inside the walls of Fort George, where the governor lived. Fear gripped Manhattan. The suspected arsonists were the New York slaves. Two hundred slaves in all were arrested and tried for conspiracy to burn down the town, kill the white men, and take the women. It was known as the Conspiracy of 1741 or the Slave Insurrection of 1741. Most of the convicted were hanged or burned, but it was also said that some were taken by their owners and chained to Execution Rocks and drowned.

Another, more oft-repeated legend of how the rocks got their name includes the same punishment, but for different victims. This legend takes place instead during the Revolutionary times (April 19, 1775–September 3, 1783, for those of you not sure of your history dates). Great Britain and its thirteen colonies (allied with France) were at war. The British Red Coats and the American colonists had a different view on how things should be run, and colonists wanted their independence. As in all wars, people are not on the friendliest of terms and to get their point across when people were captured on either side, they were often tortured. At that time executions were usually public, but it is said that at times the British opted for a less public setting to avoid more emotional upset with the rebels. According to nautical historian Andrea Watson, the British would take prisoners to this tiny island and chain them at low tide to hooks that were buried deep into the rocks. Then the prisoners would have twelve long hours to watch the tide slowly rise as, inch by inch, they came closer to a terrible death. This must have played horrible mind games on the chained prisoners, who knew there was no escape and that no amount of screaming or squirming could change their watery fate. Silenced by the waves, the victim's lifeless bodies were left there, and the exposure to the water, wind, salt, and marine life dining on them left their bones exposed and discolored. Their skeletons would be left there to further haunt the next up for their demise. (Sometimes as many as twenty men were chained to the rock to drown in a mass execution.) Some say the condemned souls are "chained" to the island and cannot be released, as they are waiting for their retribution.

Some believe, however, that the British did get their just due karma during that time. As General Washington was retreating from Manhattan to White Plains, the Red Coats got wind of it and tried to squash Washington's men by sending a boatload of Brits to intercept and capture the retreating ship. The race was under way. But the sound, being a busy shipping lane, caused the Brits to steer too close to Execution Rocks and the submerged jagged rocks "executed" their ship and made mincemeat out of it. None of the British soldiers survived in the cold waters. (Maybe the skeletons below dragged them to their watery graves, or maybe the ghosts blew them toward the rocks.)

The tales of the slaves and of the American prisoners meeting their torturous demise has never been proven, but the one thing is sure: Hundreds of ships passed by there daily, and many were downed by the "execution rocks." Since this area was a highly trafficked waterway the US government decided something needed to be done to warn the ships of the dangers of this passageway. In 1809 they built a lighthouse near Sands Point. During a clear day it was great, but during bad weather it didn't do such a great job warning seamen about the dangerous reefs below.

William H. Ellis felt another means of warning was needed. In a letter dated September 25, 1838, he wrote: "In clear weather the light upon Sand's (sic) point is an excellent guide for the southern channel; but cannot be depended on when the weather is thick and boisterous; and to those passing to the northward of the reef, it affords but little assistance at any time. On this account, a light and bell upon the reef would contribute greatly to the safety of the navigation."

As with all-important things, governmental red tape gets in the way and after some ten years back and forth with the powers that be (and many other unnecessarily downed ships), on March 3, 1847, Congress finally decided they needed to build a second lighthouse. The only question was where. So the proverbially purse was opened and out popped $25,000 for the task. After looking at submissions from various architects, Boston engineer Alexander Parris was chosen. He looked over the area and thought "Execution Rocks" island would be the perfect place. After some debate, and a few other choices, the plans were set in motion for that island to be the place.

Now the law of the land at that time (since 1809) stated that government had to grant the project to the lowest bidder, rather than to the most qualified bidder. Thomas Butler was that man.

However, Butler didn't have the skills or the crew to carry out the job, so his shoddy work had to be subcontracted out, which delayed the completion of the lighthouse to May of 1849, a full year later! It took still another year for the light to be turned on, during which more boats succumbed to their fate at those dreaded rocks. One such boat was a wooden hulled merchant boat that merely grazed the rocks one winter in 1847, and went down in minutes. Only a few men survived the freezing cold winter waters.

The understanding was that once Execution Rocks Lighthouse was done, Sand's Point Lighthouse would no longer be needed, and be sent into retirement. But that never happened. Instead, to distinguish the two, the Sand's Point Lighthouse would have a fixed white light, and the Execution Rocks Light a fixed red light. And just for safe measure, a tiny hand-rung fog bell was installed for stormy weather on Execution Rocks. (That's like having a tiny bicycle bell on a motorcycle—pretty useless, but better than nothing.)

Now that the physical details of ship safety were put to rest, there was still the issue of mental peace that needed to be addressed. After all, what lightkeeper would want to stay on Execution Rocks with all that bad karma? When lightkeepers were assigned to a lighthouse, they were contracted to be stationed there for a set amount of time. If for some reason they were unhappy they could put in for a transfer, but if it wasn't granted, tough luck, that was their assignment and they'd have to rough it out.

But with the Execution Rocks Lighthouse they did something that had never been done before in the history of lighthouses. If the lightkeeper ever requested a transfer, it had to be granted immediately, no questions asked. Or as they put it so pun-fully, they didn't want any light keeper to be "chained to the island." (Yes, readers, you can moan here.)

In addition, usually lightkeepers live in a house attached to the lighthouse, but on Execution Rocks there were no living quarters, which made it even less desirable. So the man in charge of the Sands Point Lighthouse instead was given double duty and told he had to be in charge of both lighthouses. So he hired two assistants to take care of Execution Rocks, instead of himself boating back and forth. One assistant, William Craft, decided that he would brave the rumors, so he and his wife lived in the base of the lighthouse.

But shoddy work does not last long and just five years later, by 1855, the foundation of the tower was deteriorating, the landing and plaster inside needed repairs, and that rinky-dink bell needed to be replaced for a real foghorn. So another ten years of negotiation went by. Finally, after the Civil War in 1867, a keeper's quarters was built. But bad luck continued to surround this tiny island. In 1877, the north side of the island was damaged during a storm; it was repaired, but was damaged again the following year. Among other upgrades done on the lighthouse, on May 31, 1892, a flashing ten-second-interval light replaced the steady red light. And if you are going to spruce up the inside, why not the outside? On May 15, 1899, a broad brown band was painted around the middle of the Execution Rocks tower.

Finally, to give it a proper voice, the fog signal was upgraded in 1905 to an air-compressed air siren...something that could really be heard! So now we're all good on the island, right? Nope.

Disaster struck again! At noon, on a cold December day in 1918, a thick fog crept over the tower. The then lightkeeper, Peter Forget (yes, folks, that was his real name), was enjoying his lunch and noticed that the engine, which had powered the light and foghorn, had slowed down. He went outside and headed on over to the engine house to check on what was happening. It was then he realized that the engine house was engulfed in flames. He radioed for help, then quickly alerted the assistant keeper and two Navy men who were also stationed on the island. The four of them battled the behemoth fire on this small island as Navy patrol boats, nearby soldiers from Fort Slocum, and the New York City fireboat the *Cornelius W. Lawrence* came rushing in to help. Within two hours their combined efforts had put the fire out, but the damage had been done. The fire had totally destroyed the engine room and stonework, burnt out windows on the lighthouse, and scorched the living quarters. The total damage came to a whopping $13,500! They once again had to get money to restore it.

So *now* we're all good on the island, right? Nope.

Enter serial killer Carl Panzram, born 1892. According to his mother, by the age five, Carl was already a bad seed, lying and stealing. By the age of eleven, he stole some apples, cakes, and a revolver from his neighbor's home. He wound up in the Minnesota State Training School where he said in his autobiography that he was "beaten, tortured and raped by staff members, in the 'Painting House,'" which was so named because children would leave "painted with bruises." He decided to take revenge and burned the school down in 1905, but he was never caught. By his teens he was an alcoholic and a serial burglar. After joining the army he was convicted of larceny and sent to Leavenworth's US Disciplinary Barracks. The then Secretary of War William Howard Taft approved his sentence. After serving his prison time, Panzram received a dishonorable discharge. Throughout his life he was in and out of prison, doing time for arson and burglary, and used twelve different aliases. He was arrested and imprisoned all over the country, from Texas to California to Oregon to Montana, but escaped and was often on the run. At six feet tall with a broad build, he would beat prison guards to a pulp. In his 1929 autobiography, Panzram described himself as "rage personified."

When he was sentenced to seven years in prison in Oregon State Penitentiary in Salem, he did sixty-one days in solitary confinement then managed to escape once again. On September 18, 1917, after a shootout, an arrest, and another escape, he hopped on a train and headed eastbound toward New York in 1920. That's where his evil went full tilt and his murder spree began.

In 1920, Panzram decided he wanted revenge on the man who first put him in prison. He broke into the New Haven, Connecticut, home of William H. Taft and stole a large amount of jewelry and bonds, along with Taft's Colt M1911 .45 caliber handgun. In his autobiography, Panzram says he stole $40,000 from Taft, but Taft reported that his wife's jewelry was only worth $3,000. Regardless, he had enough money to buy a yacht, a yacht he called the *Akista*, under the alias of John O'Leary. He sailed this floating chamber to City Island in New York City, then he carried out his sick plan. He described it this way: "I figured it would be a good plan to hire a few sailors to work for me, get them out to my yacht, get them drunk, commit sodomy on them, rob them and then kill them. This I done."

The murder weapon was Taft's revolver. He tied rocks to the corpses and tossed them into the waters off of Execution Rocks, where many a soldier had died centuries before. His killing spree of sailors only ended because the *Akista* ran aground and sank near Atlantic City, while his last two potential victims were on board. Luckily they escaped to parts unknown and they were never heard from again. Unfortunately, Panzram fled before anyone knew what despicable deeds he had done. He later confessed to killing ten sailors.

Panzram got arrested several more times for gun possession and robbery. He then headed to Africa, where he burned down a rig he worked on, raped and killed several young boys (feeding some of their bodies to crocodiles), and then committed more murders. It wasn't until August 30, 1928, when he was arrested in Baltimore, Maryland, for stealing a radio and some jewelry, that he voluntarily confessed to killing those boys and others. He also admitted to contemplating mass killings and wanting to poison a city's water supply with arsenic. He was sentenced to twenty-five years to life. But after he beat to death a prison laundry foreman with an iron bar on June 20, 1929, he was sentenced to death by hanging.

With his twisted mind he reveled in this and refused appeals. He berated activist groups opposed to his death sentence. He wrote, "The only thanks you and your kind will ever get from me for your efforts on my behalf is that I wish you all had one neck and that I had my hands on it." On death row, with absolutely no remorse he confessed, "In my lifetime I have murdered 21 human beings, I have committed thousands of burglaries, robberies, larcenies, arsons, and, last but not least, I have committed sodomy on more than 1,000 male human beings. For all these things I am not in the least bit sorry." He admitted to killing all of the sailors and told of their brutalized bodies at the bottom of Execution Rocks. He was hanged on September 5, 1930, at the age of thirty-eight in Leavenworth, Kansas. As the execution was about to take place, he refused the traditional black hood that is placed over the head of the prisoner. So defiant was he to the end that he spat in the executioner's face. His last words were, "Hurry it up, you Hoosier bastard! I could kill a dozen men while you're screwing around!" His body is buried in Leavenworth Penitentiary Cemetery. His grave is not marked with his vile name but only by prison number 31614. In 1970 his journal and letters were released under the title *Killer: A Journal of Murder*. Films were made of his life as well. Some says his evil spirit lurks on Execution Rocks.

This island just seems to want to be left alone of human influence. And on December 5, 1979, it got its way. With solar panels the lighthouse and light keeper's quarters became fully automated, and has not been regularly inhabited by living beings since.

But even an unruly deserted island with nothing more than ghosts and a working lighthouse needs upkeep. Upkeep costs money, so in 2007 the Department of Interior no longer wanted to be responsible for this unruly child and basically put the island up for adoption. Only one brave couple, Craig Morrison and Linell Lukesh from Philadelphia, stepped forward. Motivated by a passion to preserve lighthouses, and to offer a historic place the public

Execution Rocks is surrounded by tales of torture, fires, shipwrecks, skeletons, and ghosts, and is known as a dumping ground for a serial killer's victims. The lighthouse was occupied for centuries but as of December 5, 1979, the island became fully automated with solar power and has not been inhabited since, except for brave souls who want to spend a night.

Photo courtesy of Historically Significant Structures, Inc.

could enjoy and learn from, they formed a 501(c)(3) nonprofit organization called Historically Significant Structures, Inc. The US government gladly donated the property to their nonprofit organization! The pair redid the interior, added new walls, gave it a new paint job, and fixed windows. They went as far as their money and fundraising efforts could stretch.

But it takes a lot to keep a lighthouse going—to the tune of about $1.2 million for all the upgrades needed—you know, simple things like running water, electricity, maybe even a working bathroom, and the like. In the meantime, the infamous history of Execution Rocks kept circulating.

Enter the Travel Channel. In 2009, on a show called *Ghost Adventures*, the Execution Rocks Lighthouse became internationally known when it was featured on their show about the paranormal. In the show Zak Bagans, the lead ghost hunter, interviews the site owner, Craig Morrison. Craig related stories that "screams of the condemned men chained to the rocks could be heard by people on the shore of Long Island" (sound travels far over water). He also revealed that a psychic contacted him via email saying that there was an aggressive male presence at the lighthouse. Could it be that of Carl Panzram? Zak and his crew were going to try to find out that night. But in the meantime, they interviewed former lighthouse keepers.

Former lighthouse keeper Hector Barsali (1961–1962) said he never saw a ghost, but he periodically smelled the scent of flowers at the top of the lighthouse. He couldn't make sense of it because there was no grass or flowers on the island.

Former lighthouse keeper Dave Hall (1978–1979) said that during a number of his night shifts he would stay awake by watching TV. He would lie down on the couch in the corner in the keeper's quarters. On many occasions when he tried to get up, he felt a pressure pushing down on his chest, keeping him pinned down on the couch. While they only lasted a few seconds to a minute, he felt the time was endless. (This author notes that her son and friend who once stayed at a haunted campground in Pennsylvania both experienced the same pinned-down feeling in the guest quarters, and said it was the scariest feeling they ever experienced. They described it like almost being smothered.)

After the interviews, Zak and his crew were left alone on the island to stay overnight and see what they could uncover. They marked a black tape letter X on the spots where eyewitnesses claimed paranormal encounters. They had six cameras: One in the first-floor keeper's quarters, one viewpoint camera looking up the stairs to the keeper's quarters, one in the attic, two in the lighthouse (one looking up the steps and one looking down), and one on the helicopter pad so they could see if any ghostly figures were approaching from the outside. They also had a variety of ghost-tracking machines, such as digital thermometers, EMF (electromagnetic field) meters, handheld digital video cameras, audio recorders, the Ovilus device point-of-view cameras, and infrared night vision cameras, all in an effort to capture the tortured ghosts on camera. To get the ghosts to come out they'd taunt them (the author has tried this in another known ghost location, and it worked! Apparently, ghosts do not have a sense of humor.) The crew was also looking for Fortean phenomena such as equipment malfunctioning, battery drainage, voltage spikes, cold spots, sudden temperature changes, unexplained noises such as loud banging, orbs on camera, and, of course, actually seeing a ghost on the spot. They also use their own bodies as indicators—one of the camera guys said he felt something pass through him.

The results: Zak's ghost box goggles registered that spirits said the word "remote," then "camera," then the word "me" after asked who caused the sudden loud bang sound they had just heard. The EMF meter spiked in the middle of the floor in the keeper's bedroom, followed by the word "drink" and the word "mercury." Later it was found out that one lightkeeper had died by drinking mercury. Zak remembered a storage tank he had seen earlier with the words "Caution Mercury Poison" written on it that rested over a freshwater cistern that contained the keeper's household water. (Zak's conclusion was that the dripping mercury tank unintentionally poisoned the water.) It is a logical conclusion; however, medium and paranormal expert Lynne Sutherland Olson wrote in her paranormal blog that that same ghost that said the words "drink" and "mercury" to Zak told her "that he intentionally committed suicide by adding mercury to his nightcap because he was upset over a girl leaving him before he took the job as a light keeper." So the suicidal lightkeeper was depressed, isolated, drank too much, and decided to commit suicide, and his ghost was stuck in the lighthouse. (The author cannot vouch for whose abilities to communicate with the other side are more accurate, only that these are some encounters with the paranormal that have been documented.) The ghost hunting show ended with Zak taunting the serial killer, Panzram, and moments later his camera dying for a few seconds.

Does any of this prove the tales that surround this island? Nothing is definitive, but when you factor in the eyewitness accounts, that Panzram killed those sailors and dumped their bodies there, and that there were fires, shipwrecks, and deaths on and around the island, it doesn't add up to a happy place.

One thing is for sure: This island is here to stay. From October 22 to November 2, 2012, when Hurricane Sandy, the deadliest and most destructive hurricane of the 2012 Atlantic hurricane season hit, causing the loss of 285 people and $70 million in damage, Execution Rocks Lighthouse and quarters had just been redone. Although the land portion of the island was submerged, the house and tower sustained no interior damage! That's one determined place.

So how brave and determined are you? If you truly believe that none of this happened, then a night at the lighthouse should be nothing more than an adventure on an "infamous island."

But if you do believe souls that have overstayed their welcome might snuggle into bed with you and you would like to see if they decide to bare their "truths" to you while there, you can book an overnight stay between Memorial Day and Labor Day. But beware: This is not a five-star hotel. According to the official Historically Significant Structures website, www.lighthouserestorations.org, "There is no water or electricity on the island, so plan accordingly." (They're still raising money to get that working.) If you decide to brave an overnight stay, you must provide your own food, bedding, and transportation, and there are no refunds. But one thing is for sure—it will be a night to remember!

CHAPTER 14

The Mysteries of the
Putnam Valley Stone Chambers

Depending who you talk to, the Stone Chambers have been a mystery for either hundreds or thousands of years. There are several theories surrounding the Stone Chambers, but one thing is for sure: Someone or some being has left hundreds of them scattered around the Putnam Valley area to explore. In fact, Putnam Valley (on the East bank of the Hudson River just north of Westchester, or about a seventy-minute train ride from Manhattan, for non-city folks) has the largest concentration of these chambers in North America. Over two hundred stone chambers existed at one point, now there are approximately only one hundred still standing.

Gary Becker, a Hudson Valley resident, is a man of many hats. He's not only an Oscar-winning animator, but also has a passion for local history and loves the mystery surrounding the chambers. He explained:

Each chamber has its own earthly tones and is unique. These chambers were built for a reason, but nothing definitive is known about their history. They have a couple of different architectural styles; some are flat fronted, some have corridors, some are underground, some have drill marks, some have smoothly cut stones, and metal rings attached to the walls inside, and some have inscriptions. But even though all the chambers vary slightly, they are all made from large stones; most have seven slab stones for roofs and are usually built on bedrock. But the most distinguishing common denominator is all of them have these huge slab rocks that fit together so precisely no mortar was needed when building them. (Although recent homeowners who have them on their property have modified them with brick and mortar.) They are quite cool to see, and there is a map showing the location of all the chambers.

Donna Savino, a Hudson Valley historian, is a chamber hunter. She researches, surveys, and measures the chambers and logs them for Putnam County. Savino explains, "The stone chambers are fragile and are being destroyed at a steady rate...they are part of history. When the first English settlers came to New England, they discovered many of these chambers." But many chambers have unfortunately been bulldozed. Depending on who you talk to, "some people feel they should be preserved as part of history, while others feel they are useless and can be destroyed."

But why destroy them before you know the answers that lie within? That's like throwing out a puzzle when you've only seen an eyeball on the face! That is why experts are constantly examining them and many organizations are fighting to keep them protected.

According to Becker, "Some chambers have been reported to be ancient, based on carbon 14 dating of charcoal. Some chambers allow viewing of specific horizon events, such as solstices, equinoxes, rising of Pleiades, which basically means in layman's terms that many of the chambers were used as calendars. When the sun hit them, the people knew it was season change." (Of course, it would seem one would only need to look out a window and see snow and realize it's winter.) But the argument goes, that since this was before clocks and calendars that was their way of knowing.

According to the book *Celtic Mysteries* by Philip Imbrono, these stone huts have perplexed researchers of the paranormal and archeologists for decades, as well. (Many local groups, however, feel that his theory is not in good standing with a lot of the local Putnam preservation groups.)

The Double Chamber (located on Oscawana Lake Road just off the side of the road and down about fifteen feet, across from the Putnam Valley Elementary School), for example, "is the largest anomaly in Putnam Valley with a reading of negative 320 gamma degrees magnetivity" according to Beckern English this means that, in electric fields, there are alpha rays (heavy, positively charged particles) and beta rays (light, negatively charged electrons), both of which can be deflected by electric fields, but gamma rays have no electric charge and therefore cannot be deflected.

"Which means," said Becker, "that the level of magnetic field in that chamber can reverse the needle on a compass or, in other words, the level is strong enough to counter the local Earth's magnetic field when a compass is held directly over the center of the anomaly. It can even stop a watch." (The only anomaly higher than the Double Chamber in New York is that of red-granite Balancing Rock—a 60-ton rock balanced on a ring of smaller stones on route 121/116 in North Salem in Westchester—which has a 400 gamma reading. There are a couple of signs by the rock that explain how

Most stone chambers are single. Here is a rare double chamber located on Oscawana Lake Road down the side of the highway. It is across the street from the Putnam Valley Elementary School, hidden from view, but a trained eye knowing what to look for can find it in the woods.

it formed. One theory is that a glacier in the Ice Age deposited it, while another says it could be a ceremonial stone erected by the Celts, who visited 2,000 years ago; even with that rock there is no certainty as to its origin.)

So, what does all this mean? Possibly that each chamber of the Double Chamber could have a different purpose. According to *Celtic Mysteries*, "The purpose of these (Double) chambers are for the setting sun, and the other chamber is a ritual chamber...the activity found in this chamber is both UFO and paranormal activity."

To really examine the Double Chamber, you need a flashlight even in the daylight, and if you're tall, a hardhat might not be a bad idea, either. Each of the chambers is about the size of a large walk-in closet, with a really low ceiling. The left chamber is the larger one, with an opening 5 feet, 7 inches high, and 5 feet, 3 inches wide, and a depth of 22.83 feet. The right chamber is 4 feet, 5 inches high, 4 feet, 3 inches wide, and 17.75 feet deep.

They're damp inside and each has a dirt floor. Inside are faint carvings on the ceiling. Burnt candles have been found lying on the dirt floor as if someone camped there for the night. (An hour after visiting the Double Chamber, this author—who is like the Energizer Bunny—had a sudden energy zap in the middle of the day, to the point that she couldn't keep her eyes open. Apparently this is a common effect of this particular chamber.)

So what theories surround these cave-like dwellings?

COLONIAL ROOT CELLARS

The first theory (and most popular) is that they were colonial root cellars used to store food. Since the Hudson Highlands area has tons of rock slabs and boulders, those who believe this theory feel it was easy to utilize the stones to build storage units. This theory states that the only reason the chambers face east was because the farmers needed the morning light to use the cellars. According to Jim Baker, a Putnam environmentalist and planning chairman for the town of Kent, "A local group of men would make ramps of earth and used oxen to pull the stones up." Baker further goes on to say that there is a written interview with a local Putnam Valley farmer, Lucas Barger, who says his ancestors actually helped settle the area, and that the information of how the chambers were built was passed down to him from his relatives. If this theory is true, it dates the construction of the chambers to 250 years ago. This is the popular or conventional view that is taught in Putnam Valley schools. Many Putnam residents don't get the big hype made out of these chambers.

To many locals, it's just a place for the kids to hang out, store trash, and paint graffiti. Henry Grosskamp of Dutchess says, "My family used to store apples and vegetables that they grew in there, but now it's useless. I'm waiting for the day the town widens the road and knocks it down." But the local historical societies, libraries, hikers, environmentalists, and even some politicians are not sold on this theory.

These people argue that, if they are root cellars, why are there no records of them being made by colonists? The hearsay of a relative telling a relative is not fact. Others argue that there is no account of them being built because they were insignificant buildings. As Mrs. Sallie Sypher, a former Putnam County historian, says, "They didn't write about their outhouses, either!" But just because they weren't written about doesn't mean that they aren't a historical part of the Putnam charm and should be saved.

Supposedly there was a writing of one colonist who reported not only that he found one chamber already made on his property, but he was told by a local priest to avoid it. This document can no longer be found.

There are so many unanswered questions surrounding the chambers. If they were root cellars, then why are some of them entirely above ground, which would be useless for storing food? Why aren't there any hinges for door attachments? And if there were no doors, how was the food protected from animals or sealed for insulation to protect it from extreme temperatures? It's possible any wooden doors may have disintegrated over time. Also, there is no ventilation in these chambers, which would mean that produce would rot inside the chambers from mold and the buildup of ethylene gas. Without ventilation fruits ripen faster and simply wouldn't last long.

The lower Hudson Valley was one of the last areas to be settled because of all the hills, which would mean it was a lousy area to grow crops. Nevertheless, some have speculated the Irish potato farmers grew crops and built the chambers to store their potatoes. If that's the case, then why would so many chambers be in an area where the least amount of produce is grown, unless of course it was to preserve what was so scarce? And why weren't the food chambers uniform across the whole state?

Sheep and dairy farming was the big thing in the Putnam area. Maybe they were shelters for the shepherds. The questions are as endless as a class filled with kindergarten students wanting to know when playtime is.

In his book *The Search for America*, Salvatore Michael Trento wrote that the "Putnam Chambers appear to be the congregated structures of a social community; they are strangely different from any that have been built since colonial times," suggesting they are not food storage chambers.

The late Martin Brech, the former Hudson Valley coordinator for the New England Antiquities Research Association (NAARA. org), said, "It is preposterous that some farmer would—or could— haul multi-ton slabs of granite just to make a shed. You don't need to go to these lengths for a storage space, you only do something like this for religious purposes." That leads us to the next theory.

CELTIC-DRUID TEMPLES

The second theory is that the chambers are Celtic-Druid temples, placing them at about 2,500 years old. Those who think along these lines say they were built as an extension of the same Neolithic culture (i.e., Stonehenge) that built passage tombs in Ireland. Once a year, during the spring equinox (March 20), when the daytime and nighttime are approximately the same length all over the planet, the rays of the sun can go directly through the doorway of the chambers onto the back wall, illuminating the interior. According to the *New York Times*, "Archaeoastronomy, the alignment of structures with the heavens, is usually associated with such ancient wonders as Machu Picchu in Peru or the New Grange Burial Chamber" in Boyne Valley in Ireland's Ancient East, which is 5,200 years old.

Many of the Putnam chambers are aligned to certain stars that are associated with the ancient Druids, and some have intricate carvings on the walls. And as many history books reveal, European explorers visited the America's about 1,000 years before Columbus got there in 1492, and the construction of these chambers match the constructions they had that were a significant part of their religion. To add further credence to this theory, a Putnam Valley student on a school trip to a local chamber found a hand knife under a rock with the shape and design that matched that of the Druids. (Of course, who's to say that he and his friends didn't purchase it from an antique shop and plant it there, knowing there would be a school trip the next day to look like a hero for finding it? But until we have the name of this student, this story is just hearsay.)

Similar stone chambers also exist in Connecticut, Vermont, and New Hampshire. Mystery Hill in Salem, New Hampshire, so named by William Goodwin, an antiquarian and insurance proponent who believes in the Celtic theory of the chambers, purchased this "ignored" site from a colonial family named Pattees. He believed this New Hampshire chamber was built by "Culdees," Irish Monks who had been fleeing the Vikings over 2,000 years ago. In 1956 the site became the property of the Stone family. The Stones christened their site, "America's Stonehenge" (get it?), although the only thing the two sites have in common is that they are both made of stone. Many people came from around the world to see the site and try to figure out its origins. (Folks it's all in the marketing!) In his book, *America B.C.*, Barry Fell, a Harvard marine biology professor, claimed "America's Stonehenge" and other chambers have similar inscriptions in them identified as Ogam, an ancient Irish Language.

"America's Stonehenge" is an international tourist attraction for curiosity seekers. One sign outside reads, in part, "These intriguing chambers hold a fascinating story and could be remnants of a pre-Viking or even Phoenician civilization."

But just like the chambers in Putnam, the origins have never really been determined, although some radiocarbon analysis has said there was human occupation in that area dating back to 2000 BC. But human occupation doesn't mean the chambers were built then.

Sam Oliverio, a former Putnam County legislator, holds to an alternative theory. "It's not far-fetched," he says, "to think that instead of 1492, maybe in 500 AD, explorers came ashore and built them." Oliverio over the years has fought to save the chambers when people wanted to knock them down. They would question his motives and say, "Hey Sam, what do you want to save a root cellar for?"

Still others who believe this theory feel that more recent Celtic descendants may have built them, (Irish are one of the six Celtic nations. You can be Celtic and not Irish.) From 1837 to 1842 when the first Croton Dam in Yorktown was built (it's now an underwater landmark in Yorktown), hundreds of Italian and Irish mason workers were brought to the area to build the dam. Many of these immigrants stayed and some feel that the Irish built these chambers to resemble the ones back home. (Note: The dams were built prior to the Irish Potato Famine of 1845–1852, so they weren't hording potatoes in the chambers out of fear or habit.)

Martin Brech, who also lectured and gave tours on the chambers, and taught at Westchester Community College on ancient and medieval philosophy (and was living in an unusual dwelling himself in a geodesic dome house built around a tree in Mahopac), believed that they were "spiritual centers for ancients who once lived in Putnam." He said he once spent a cold December night in a Kent chamber and had a "profound mystical experience at sunrise." But not all spirituality has to come from the Celtics.

NATIVE AMERICAN TEMPLES

The third theory is that they are Native American temples, dealing with spirituality and linking them to Mother Earth. This would date them back over 10,000 years. Those who believe this theory argue that the "stone slab roofs are not Colonial in nature, that no cement was used and the stones were not quarried with the use of metal drills." This theory says these chambers are like the New

England version of kiva (not to be mistaken for a kiwi, which is a fruit). A kiva is a room used by modern Puebloans for religious rituals, many of them associated with the Kachina belief system. Among the modern Hopi and most other Pueblo peoples, kivas are square-walled and aboveground, and are used for spiritual ceremonies. The Kachina belief system dates back to approximately AD 1250, while kiva-like structures occurred much earlier.

Some organizations, like the New England Antiquities Research Association (NEARA.org), have financed scientific research for some stone chambers (like the Upton Chamber in Massachusetts) using a technique called optically stimulated luminescence (OSL), which involves taking samples of soil from behind the lowest stones in the wall, at three different locations in the chamber. The samples were sent to a lab and the results came back dating the Upton chamber from AD 1625 to AD 1350. However, samples taken outside the chamber only resulted in an OSL reading of 55 to 175 years old. According to the site *Quaternary Geochronology*:

> The Upton Chamber OSL sampling results are challenging to interpret because there are mixtures in the samples of both younger and older grains that likely result from human modification, root or soil processes, animal bioturbation (i.e. ants and worms), and/or partial bleaching. The ages were determined using the lowest component of the finite mixture model as applied to a distribution of quartz grains. Further research may enable us to determine whether older components are of anthropomorphic or geological origin.

Yet this OSL technique has been commonly used at other pre-European contact archeological sites through the United States. The land on which this Upton Chamber was built was occupied by the Nipmuc Indians until AD 1704 and is said to be of significance to this theory applying to all of the chambers.

Salvatore Michael Trento, who studied at Oxford and worked for the National Geographic Society and studied ancient megaliths all over the world, created the Middletown Archaeological Research Center. He decided to give the Putnam Chambers a thorough investigation; with a large team of knowledgeable people he methodically excavated twelve chambers throughout the Northeast. His belief was that American Indians built them. But he said he found it "extraordinarily unusual that there are no artifacts there." He said, there is "always something left behind, but these chambers have literally been swept clean." He feels these chambers are "not made by Celts or aliens." He is intrigued that, while "every bit of non-Indian architecture in this country can be traced back to models in Europe, everything from stone walls to barns. . . there is nothing like these chambers in Europe." Although he believes they were built by Native Americans, he still cannot draw a definitive conclusion. As he puts it, "After all these years, no one has any idea what they are." Which leads us to our alien friends.

PORTALS FOR ALIENS AND UFOS

When in doubt, let's get beings from other planets involved. According to Imbrono's *Celtic Mysteries*, as well as a DVD seminar on the local chambers, some chambers were portals for extraterrestrials. This would be the fourth theory.

"In Europe," according to Imbrono, "these same type of constructions are known to appear along the lines of energy and power." So are the ones found in Putnam Valley: "Drawing to them appearances of odd lights and UFOs. Scientific evidence shows them to be centered on weird, magnetic field anomalies." Such as the magnetic fields found in the Double Chamber. Dr. Bruce Cornet, a UFO expert, brought a proton procession magnetometer to measure the magnetic field in four different chambers. He reported that he got the "strangest readings" he'd ever gotten in this area. According to Cornet, "each stone chamber had a significant magnetic pull right in front of the door." He concluded that the magnetic pulls place these chambers much older than Colonial times. He further stated, "These chambers could be sensing platforms to search for extraterrestrial visitation." Ever notice that aliens never pick a place like Times Square to show up in? And it's always some remote place that they can enter unnoticed? The same seems to be true with the paranormal.

MEETING HUBS FOR THE PARANORMAL

In Brewster, a small chamber located on a dark and desolate road known as Reservoir Road is said to be the site of several reports of encounters with unusual beings. One unnamed woman reportedly took a picture of a ghostly hooded figure in front of that stone chamber. Many others who have taken photos while visiting that chamber report strange images like floating globes of light (or orbs) that appeared on film when the pictures were developed. Although none of those people saw the orbs while at the chamber, the apparitions are seen clearly in their pictures. (Could it just be floating dirt on a camera lens?) This paranormal activity is the fifth theory, and some feel it is still a haunting ground used by those who have passed to the other side.

Of course, the only way to "prove" paranormal activity is with a psychic. Enter Janet Russell, psychic and TV show producer. During the spring of 1998, she visited the area near Magnetic Mine Road in Brewster and shared her experience.

A group of us went up to Brewster on May 23, 1998. I had never been up there before so I was interested in what was happening there. Well anyway, we sat around for quite a while, when one of the fellas said, "Hey, I want to show you something." So a few of us went with my friend to what was called the Stone Caves or Caverns. Since I am a psychic I do feel certain energies, well anyway, we all went over to this spot. We got out of the car as soon as I approached what was the doorway to the cave. I all of a sudden felt a drastic change in the temperature. It went from being comfortable to what felt to me like I was in an ice-cold freezer. The hair on my body stood up, it was very strange to say the least. Well I immediately got the strange feeling that I was being watched by what I felt was a Bigfoot. So me being as brave as I could (LOL), I went directly back to the car. I did not like the energy at that spot. My friends stayed outside the car, but they said they saw what looked like a shadow of a Bigfoot. Well while I was seated in the car, I just glanced over into the woods and lo and behold, I saw what looked like yellow piercing eyes staring back at me. But it was only instantaneous. I saw the eyes in two different spots at the same time. Well, my buddies were still outside surveying what they saw and felt, I still was in the car (Brave One Me). I happened to look down the darkened road and all of a sudden I saw what looked like globes bouncing up and down the road about 1000 feet in front of me. With what looked like a green aura or being of some kind. We were there about an hour and it was a very strange feeling, I did not feel that the energy was positive at all, almost evil.

Evil energies could also be the occult practice of witchcraft, which brings us to our next theory.

WICCA GROUPS

The Putnam area is known to have a lot of Wicca activity, which has a lot to do with energy fields and rituals. So this sixth theory surrounds the belief in what was once called witchcraft, which was associated with evil (in the middle 1600s) but then it became Wicca in 1954 (also termed Pagan Witchcraft), which is generally used for good purposes. Some say that the Wicca groups or cults could have built these chambers to perform their sacred rituals that they like to keep secret.

In 1992, a man claimed to have encountered a white robed figure on Route 301 coming out of that chamber. When he went to investigate, the figure signaled him to leave. Other robed beings (sometimes including dwarves) were accompanied by hooded Viking-like entities. (Now that's a visual!)

Another chamber on Route 301—in Kent right off of Forest Court—is known as a corbel chamber, which is right there smack on the side of the highway. According to *Celtic Mysteries*, the purpose of this Kent chamber was to act as a channel for the natural energy of mother earth. The activity of this chamber was reported as paranormal. (When this author visited the Kent chamber someone had left their card and a red feather.) The energy in this chamber is very positive and makes one feel energized. This is a happy gateway.

STORAGE FOR REVOLUTIONARY WAR AMMUNITION

The seventh theory is that the chambers were used during the Revolutionary War for ammunition storage. The proponents of this theory feel that since the chambers have heavy side walls and slab roofs, some have "paved" floors, and some were semi-subterranean, these chambers could have easily been camouflaged with brush quickly if the enemy was coming, and would be a perfect hideout for storage of weapons. While some chambers are near frequented roads, many of them are hidden in the valleys. Those who believe this theory say the proximity to Continental Village in Cold Spring, Peekskill, and other Revolutionary War sites makes this a plausible reason for the chambers. And considering that Route 301 was used extensively during the Revolutionary War period and a lot of the chambers are located near there, this theory seems highly plausible.

Whatever theory suits your fancy, no one believes these chambers were meant to be lived in. They were either food storage, portals, hideouts for ammunition or runaway slaves, or even sailors and Phoenician traders looking to get a little shut-eye and out of the hot sun. There is enough variety of chambers to support all these views, hence the ongoing debate and curiosity for those who like to solve puzzles. If you decide to engage in chamber hunting, respect the chambers as you would an antique you'd have to pay for if you broke it, and keep your eyes and mind open to the clues that may have not been discovered by all the professionals who have come before you. Who knows? Maybe you'll be the lucky adventurer in this world of myths and mysteries to unravel what others could not.

BIBLIOGRAPHY

IS THAT AN ALLIGATOR IN THE SEWER?

"Alligator Found in Uptown Sewer." *New York Times,* February 10, 1935, p. F29. http://sewergator.com/news/nyt19350210.htm.

Daley, Robert. *The World Beneath the City.* Philadelphia: Lippincott, 1959. www.sewergator.com/lit/world_beneath_the_city.htm.

Emery, David. "NYC Official: Send Gator Back to Sewer! Environmental Chief Worries about Critter's Chances of Survival." AP, Fox News, June 20, 2001. http://urbanlegends.about.com/od/alligators/a/alligator_ny2.htm.

Mock, Richard. "On the Incidence of Alligators and Hard Times." *New York Times,* June 19, 1982, p. 24. www.sewergator.com/news/nyt19820619.htm.

Quindlen, Anna. "Debunking the Myth of Subterranean Saurians." *New York Times,* May 19, 1982, p. 3. www.sewergator.com/news/nyt19820519.htm.
Speed, Barbara. "Yes, They Really Have Found Alligators in the New York Sewer System," *City Metric*, August 12, 2014. www.citymetric.com/yes-they-really-have-found-alligators-new-york-sewer-system-102.

http://lists.gatorhole.com/pipermail/croclist/2002-November/000102.html.

http://sewergator.com/news/nyt19820519.htm.

http://urbanlegends.about.com/od/alligators/a/sewer_gators.htm.

www.weirdus.com/states/new_york/bizarre_beasts/alligators_in_the_sewers/index.php.

FAMOUS GHOSTS OF THE DAKOTA

Adams III, Charles J. *New York City Ghost Stories.* Reading, PA: Exeter House Books, 1996.

Faraci, Derek. "The Haunting of New York's Infamous Dakota Building," *13th Floor*, July 21, 2016. www.the13thfloor.tv/2016/07/21/the-haunting-of -new-yorks-infamous-dakota-building/.

Fowler, Brittany. "15 Crazy Facts about New York's Most Exclusive Buildings," *Business Insider*, August 27, 2015. www.businessinsider.com/15-crazy-facts -about-nycs-dakota-building-2015-8.

http://cityroom.blogs.nytimes.com/2007/10/29/answers-about-haunted-new -york.

http://en.wikipedia.org/wiki/Mark_David_Chapman.

www.gothamcityinsider.com/2007/08/dakota-new-york-citys-most-legendary .html.

www.imdb.com/title/tt0063522/trivia?tr0729544.

www.nyc-architecture.com/UWS/UWS017.htm.

THE MONTAUK PROJECT

Berlitz, Charles, and William Moore. *The Philadelphia Experiment—Project Invisibility.*

"The Carl Allen Letters," The Philadelphia Experiment from A–Z. www.de173. com/carl-allen/.

Carlson, Gil. The Montauk Project. Blue Planet Project (ebook), 2017.

Gethard, Chris. *Weird New York.* New York: Sterling Publishing Inc, 2005.

Gonzales, Dave. "Inside the Real-Life Time-Travel Experiment that Inspired 'Stranger Things,'" Thrillist Entertainment, August 30, 2016. www.thrillist

.com/entertainment/nation/stranger-things-true-story-montauk-project
-philadelphia-experiment#.

Heidner, E.P. "9/11, WTC7 and the Black Eagle Trust: How Bank of New
York May Have Laundered $240 Billion," COTO Report, June 3, 2011.

Nichols, Preston. Interview, September 23, 2010.

———. *The Montauk Project: Experiments in Time*. Westbury, NY: Skybooks,
June 1992.

———, and Peter Moon. *Pyramids of Montauk: Exploration in Consciousness*.
Westbury, NY: Skybooks, 1995.

Turner, Joe. "The Philadelphia Experiment: What They Didn't Want You To
Know." http://viewzone2.com/philadelphiax.html.

X, Commander. *The Philadelphia Experiment Chronicles: Exploring the Strange
Case of Alfred Bielek and Dr. M. K. Jessup*. Inner Light Publications & Global
Communications, 1994.

www.bielek.com.

http://conspiracyguy.wordpress.com/2008/08/04/the-montauk-monster.

https://coto2.wordpress.com/2011/06/03/911-wtc7-and-the-black-eagle
-trust-how-bank-of-new-york-may-have-laundered-240-billion/.

http://www.crystalinks.com/montauk.html.

www.v-j-enterprises.com/montauk.html.

TYPHOID MARY: THE KILLER COOK

Leavitt, Judith Walzer. "The Most Dangerous Woman: Typhoid Mary: Villain
or Victim?" PBS Broadcast, Oct. 12, 2004.

———. "Typhoid Mary: Villain or Victim?" *NOVA*. www.pbs.org/wgbh/nova/
typhoid/mary.html.

Robin, Josh. "The Secret of North Brother Island: The Abandoned NYC Island Where Typhoid Mary Was Held Captive," *The Daily Beast*, December 29, 2017.

Rosenberg, Jennifer. "Biography of Typhoid Mary," *ThoughtCo.*, March 29, 2018. http://history1900s.about.com/od/1900s/a/typhoidmary.htm.

Schubach, Alanna. "Long Off Limits, North Brother Island May Finally Be Open to the Public," *Live*, November 2, 2016. www.brickunderground.com/live/visit-north-brother-island.

www.thedailybeast.com/the-secret-of-north-brother-island-the-abandoned -new-york-city-island-where-typhoid-mary-was-held-captive?ref=scroll.

THE LEGENDS OF HELL GATE

Apuzzo, Robert. *The Endless Search for the HMS* Hussar: *New York's Legendary Treasure Shipwreck*. New York: R & L Publishing, 2008.

Evelly, Jeanmarie. "Astoria Group Wants to Light up Hell Gate Bridge," Astoria & Long Island City Transportation, December 25, 2013. www.dnainfo.com/new-york/20131225/astoria/astoria-group-wants-light-up-hell-gate-bridge/.

Galiano, Rich. http://njscuba.net/sites/site_treasure.html.

Healy, Ryan. "The Strange History of NYC's Mighty Hell Gate," gothamist, February 22, 2016. http://gothamist.com/2016/02/22/hell_gate_history_nyc.php.

Kilgannon, Corey. "A Bad Impression Outlasts a Bridge's New Paint," *New York Times*, March 8, 2012. https://cityroom.blogs.nytimes.com/2012/03/08/a-bad-impression-outlasts-a-bridges-new-paint/.

"New York City: Revolutionary Wreck." *New York Times*. http://query.nytimes .com/mem/archive-free/pdf?_r=1&res=9900EED81339E134BC4053 DFBF66838D649FDE.

Scardino, Albert, and Alan Finder. "Raise the HMS *Hussar*," *New York Times,* Sept. 29, 1985. www.nytimes.com/1985/09/29/weekinreview/the-region -raise-the-hms-hussar.html.

Vanderbilt, Tom. "Ship of Dreams." *New York Times,* Feb. 17, 2002. www.ny times.com/2002/02/17/nyregion/ship-of-dreams.html?pagewanted=all.

http://captbbrucato.wordpress.com/2009/05/17/new-york-citys-east-river -and-hell-gate.

http://en.wikipedia.org/wiki/Hell_Gate.

http://en.wikipedia.org/wiki/HMS_Hussar.

www.geocaching.com/seek/cache_details.aspx?guid=1791f5d9-6c7f-4efc -8977-92d2e5da4a60.

www.nan.usace.army.mil/whoweare/hellgate.pdf.

www.nytimes.com/1985/09/29/weekinreview/the-region-raise-the-hms -hussar.html.

THE MYSTERIOUS LEATHER MAN

Capo, Fran. "Ode to the Leatherman (1838–1889)," July 2018. www.francapo .com.

DeLuca, Dan. www.skyweb.net/~channy/leatherman.html.

The Road Between Heaven and Hell. The Connecticut Humanities Council Documentary, 1984. www.youtube.com/watch?v=jIIhSPI58x8&feature= player_embedded.

www.dreadcentral.com/news/34330/cold-spots-the-legend-leatherman.

www.dreadcentral.com/img/coldspots/092-04.jpg.

http://en.wikipedia.org/wiki/Leatherman.

www.leavetheleathermanalone.com/.

www.makemeknow.com/Regional/USA/CT/Legend_of_the_Old_Leather
man_185.php.

THE LAKE CHAMPLAIN MONSTER

Brown, Carl. "Samuel de Champlain Saw Them First." *Valley News,* August 9,
1978, p. 11.

Consadine, Mary. Interview, August 7, 2010.

Gibson, Walker. "The True Tale of the Essex Monster." *Valley News,* August 9,
1978, p. 9.

Lake Champlain Monster: Early 90's TV segment from either 11-13-1992 or
12-4-1991. Ripped from decaying VHS. Posted on Youtube.

Pope, Connie. "The Lake Champlain Sea Serpent: The Anatomy of a Legend."
Valley News, August 9, 1978, p. 5.

"The Lake Champlain Monster: Special Section." *Valley News,* No. 28, August
9, 1978.

Zarzynski, Joseph. "From Loch Ness to Lake Champlain." *Valley News,* August
9, 1978, p. 7.

http://en.wikipedia.org/wiki/Champ.

http://theshadowlands.net/serpent.htm#Japan.

www.strangemag.com/champ.html.

www.unmuseum.org/champ.htm.

https://video.search.yahoo.com/yhs/search;_ylt=A2KLfaKOraJbe1IAlL
cPxQt.;_ylu=X3oDMTByMjB0aG5zBGNvbG8DYmYxBHBvcwM
xBHZ0aWQDBHNlYwNzYw--?p=recent+Lake+champlain+mon
ster+sitings&fr=yhs-pty-pty_maps&hspart=pty&hsimp=yhs-pty_
maps#id=3&vid=4c87534d3c9afbd6bf4cda37cb631e43&action=view.

BIZARRE TALES OF BUCKOUT ROAD

Gethard, Chris. *Weird New York*. New York: Sterling Publishing Inc., 2005.

Lascala, Marisa. "Westchester County Urban Legend of Buckout Road in White Plains West Harrison NY to Become Movie Directed by 90201 Actor Jason Priestly," *Hudson Valley Magazine*, October 2011. www.hvmag .com/Blogs/Poptional-Reading/October-2011/Westchester-County-Urban -Legend-of-Buckout-Road-in-White-Plains-West-Harrison-NY-to-Become -Movie-Directed-By-90210-Actor-Jason-Priestley/.

Pleska, Eric. Interview, September 15, 2010.

Sciortino, Dina. "The Legend of Buckout Road: The Movie," *Patch*, Oct. 21, 2011. https://patch.com/new-york/whiteplains/legend-of-buckout-road -the-movie.

www.bedofnailz.com/buckout.html.

www.emtbravo.net/index.php?showtopic=33992.

www.facebook.com/photo.php?pid=1631057&o=all&op=1&view=all&subj= 51074668925&aid=1&id=571458433&oid=51074668925.

www.strangeusa.com/ViewLocation.aspx?locationid=7055.

http://wackywestchesterwoods.blogspot.com/2008/12/infamous-buckout -road.html.

www.weirdus.com/states/new_york/road_less_traveled/head_buckout_road/ index.php.

MCGURK'S SUICIDE BAR

"Final Rites for McGurk's Suicide Hall," Curbed.com, July 8, 2005.

"Mae West: 295 Bowery," *Mae West*, February 22, 2006, http://maewest.blog spot.com/2006/02/mae-west-295-bowery.html.

"McGurk's Suicide Hall—295 Broadway." *Daytonian in Manhattan,* September 10, 2010.

"Ready to Demolish Notorious Downtown Bowery Building," *DownTown Express,* April 2005.

Sante, Luc. *Low Life: Lures and Snares of Old New York.* New York: Farrar, Straus and Giroux, 1991.

http://theboweryboys.blogspot.com/2007/10/friday-night-fever-mcgurks -suicide-hall.html.

http://daytoninmanhattan.blogspot.com/2010/09/mcgurks-suicide-hall-295 -bowery.html.

www.downtownexpress.com/de_102/readytodemolish.html.

www.forgotten-ny.com/STREET%20SCENES/bowery/bowery.html.

http://ny.curbed.com/archives/2005/07/08/final_rites_for_mcgurks_suicide_ hall.php.

http://rob.hilluva.com/writing/McGurksSuicideHall.html.

THE BEAUTIFUL CIGAR GIRL

Burroughs, Edwin G., and Mike Wallace. *Gotham, A History of New York City to 1898.* New York: Oxford University Press, 1999.

Byrnes, Thomas. *1886 Professional Criminals of America.* New York: Chelsea House, 1969.

Geary, Rick. *The Mystery of Mary Rogers.* New York: Nantier, Beall, Minoustchine Publishing Inc., 2001.

"The Legend of Sybil's Cave, Hoboken, NJ," *Mystery and Paranormal.* http:// mysteryandparanormal.blogspot.com/2017/11/the-legend-of-sybil-cave -hoboken-nj.html.

Lenoir, Andrew. "Unsolved Murder Fascinated 1840s New York and Edgar Allan Poe," *Mental Floss*, February 24, 2017.

MacGowan, Douglass. *The Body Near the Shore*, TruTV.com.

Paul, Raymond. *Who Murdered Mary Rogers?* Englewood Cliffs, NJ: Prentice Hall, 1971.

Poe, Edgar Allan. "The Mystery of Marie Roget," reprinted in *Great Tales and Poems of Edgar Allan Poe*. New York: Pocket Books, 1951.

http://mentalfloss.com/article/92444/unsolved-murder-fascinated-1840s-new -york-and-edgar-allan-poe.

www.trutv.com/library/crime/notorious_murders/classics/mary_rogers.

The Friendly Ghost Hostess of Skene Manor

Kessler, Joanne. Interview August 8, 2010.

Smitten, Susan. *Ghost Stories of New York State*. Auburn, WA: Lone Pine Publishing International, 2004.

www.dupontcastle.com/castles/skeneman.htm.

www.skenemanor.org.

The Unlucky *General Slocum*

"*General Slocum* Disaster NYC." June 15, 1904. www.archives.gov.

Kornblum, William. *At Sea in the City: New York from the Water's Edge*. Chapel Hill, NC: Algonquin Books, 2002.

"Tales of Horror Told by Survivors; Eye-Witness Stories of Swift and Awful Panic." *New York Times*, June 16, 1904. http://query.nytimes.com/gst/ abstract.html?res=F50611FF3A5913738DDDAF0994DE405B848CF1D3.

"Van Schaick Pardoned. Captain of Ill-fated *Slocum* Is Restored to Full Citizenship." *New York Times,* December 20, 1912. http://query.nytimes .com/gst/abstract.html?res=F60811FB355E13738DDDA90A94 DA415B828DF1D3.

www.junipercivic.com/HistoryArticle.asp?nid=15.

www.suite101.com/content/the-general-slocum-disaster-a215440#ixzz10 DmTgPAj.

EXECUTION ROCKS

Caro, Robert A. *The Power Broker: Robert Moses and the Fall of New York.* New York: Alfred A. Knopf Inc., 2012.

Cochran, Barry. "Ghost Adventures – Execution Rocks Lighthouse," dailymotion.

www.dailymotion.com/video/xqhhj6 (originally aired in 2009 on the Travel Channel with host Zak Bagans).

http://lighthousemuseum.org/visit/lighthouse-boat-tours/.

www.lighthouserestorations.org

https://lynnesutherlandolson.wordpress.com/2010/09/11/execution-rocks -lighthouse/.

www.scoutingny.com/a-trip-to-execution-rocks/.

www.us-lighthouses.com/displaypage.php?LightID=456.

THE MYSTERIES OF THE PUTNAM VALLEY STONE CHAMBERS

"Balanced Rock (North Salem, NY)," *Adventures Around Putnam.* www .adventuresaroundputnam.com/day-trips-outside-putnam/balanced -rocknorth-salem-ny/.

Becker, Gary. Interview, August 29, 2007.

Imbrono, Philip, and Marianne Horrigan. *Celtic Mysteries in New England*. Woodbury, MN: Llewellyn Publications, 2000.

Kilgannon, Corey. "Putnam's Mysterious Chambers of Stone," *New York Times*, April 22, 2001.

Mahan, Shannon A., F.W. Martin, and Catherine Taylor. "Construction Ages of the Upton Stone Chamber," *Quaternary Geochronology*, May 20, 2015. www .uptonma.gov/sites/uptonma/files/uploads/upton_stone_chamber_ -_preliminary_findings.pdf.

Midgley, Polly. Interview, October 18, 2018.

Savino, Donna. Interview, August 29, 2007.

www.atlasobscura.com.

www.nytimes.com/2001/04/22/nyregion/putnam-s-mysterious-chambers-of -stone.html.

INDEX

ABOUT THE AUTHOR

PETER M. BUDRAITIS

Fran Capo is a comedienne, actress, author of twenty books, adventurer, motivational speaker, consultant, spokesperson, and six-time record holder in the *Guinness Book of World Records* as the world's fastest talking woman, clocked at 603.32 words per minute—that's eleven words per second! Her other world records include a book signing down by the wreck site of the *Titanic*, and one on the top of Mt. Kilimanjaro.

Fran has appeared on over 450 TV shows and 4,500 radio shows including her most recent appearances on *The Morning Show on 7* (Australian TV), *Entertainment Tonight*, *Fox and Friends*, *The Dr. Oz Show*, *Good Morning America*, and *Nickelodeon*. She's done peak performance training for Fortune 500 companies, the military, schools, churches, fundraisers, and private functions on every continent (including Antarctica) teaching people in a down-to-earth, humorous way "How to Have a World Record Mindset" and live a life full of passion, humor, and creativity. Her book *Hopeville: The City of Light* hit #11 on Amazon and unlocks the forty-four secrets to happiness. Her one-woman show, *Love, Laughter, and Light,* is based on these secrets. Fran has appeared on the cover of *Influential People Magazine* and in *Woman's Day* magazine.

Currently, Fran is the radio host of "Fran's World" on WestchesterTalkRadio, the TV adventure correspondent on *Live it Up!* with Donna Drake, and blogs for *TravelingMom*. She produces sold-out comedy events, and has appeared in multiple award-winning films, including *Father and Father.*

Fran is happily married to Steve, whom she had brought to the altar in handcuffs. She has one son, Spencer, a future daughter-in-law, Heather, and a stepdaughter, Jamie, as well as three cats and a sometimes live-in dog, Ruby.

Fran believes nothing is impossible and lives life to the fullest. Follow Fran on social media, or check out www.francapo.com.